Famine
A man-made disaster?

Famine
A man-made disaster?

A report for the Independent Commission
on International Humanitarian Issues

Pan Books London and Sydney

This report does not necessarily reflect the views, individually or collectively, of the members of the Independent Commission on International Humanitarian Issues (ICIHI). It is based on research carried out for ICIHI and was prepared under the supervision of its Secretariat with the guidance of the ICIHI Working Group on Disasters.

First published 1985 by Pan Books Ltd,
Cavaye Place, London SW10 9PG
© The Secretariat of the Independent Commission
on International Humanitarian Issues
ISBN 0 330 29111 4
Set in Linoterm Times New Roman by
JH Graphics Ltd, Reading
Printed and bound in Great Britain by
Cox & Wyman Ltd, Reading

The Independent Commission on International Humanitarian Issues

Contents

Foreword

Famine a man-made disaster? Instinctively one wants to believe that it is not true, that nature not man is responsible. It is far more comfortable for us all if we can continue to think of famine as being the result of drought, disease or flooding. The uncomfortable truth is that the facts point unerringly to man contributing as well to famine conditions. Nature alone cannot be held responsible.

If responsibility is not with nature, it is easiest to put the blame squarely on the ex-colonial powers. It is certainly true that the burden of responsibility does lie here, but even so that is not the whole story. Africa has not been as neglected as the famine might lead one to believe. In sub-Saharan Africa as a whole official annual aid per person amounted to about $18 a year in 1982; in the low-income semi-arid countries aid has, since the famine in the mid-1970s, reached more than $44 a head. In south Asia aid amounts to only $4.80 per person. In Africa aid finances 10 per cent of gross domestic investment and up to 80 per cent for the low-income semi-arid countries.

Against that record of aid spending there is, however, a pathetic story of the international community taking back with one hand what it is giving with the other, which puts the entire aid programme generated by drought into a different perspective. Between 1973 and 1982 sub-Saharan Africa's debt increased fivefold. In the two years 1980–82, following the oil price increases and a slump in world trade,

Africa borrowed heavily to maintain its level of imports, some essential – some far from essential. Public-debt service payments amounted to $9.9 billion in 1984 and are expected to rise to $11.6 billion a year from now until 1987.

Africa has also been hard hit by changes in world commodity prices. In 1972 it took thirty-eight tonnes of Tanzanian sisal to buy a seven tonne truck, by 1982 it took 134 tonnes. The fall in the real value of copper from Zambian mines has been 60 per cent over the last ten years. With this massive shift of trade against Africa it is true, as is argued, that aid becomes an even lonelier link to the international economy.

Comprehensive reform of international economic relationships is essential and action will help alleviate not just famine but the whole miserable saga of poverty and deprivation that is all too evident all over Africa. Famine will not, however, be eradicated even if all of the desirable international economic actions bear immediate fruit, unless the primacy of small-scale farming is restored. Unless, as is argued, the arrangements for implementing aid are shifted decisively from the large programmes to smaller ones. Unless more manageable projects can be taken over locally. Unless the institutional pro-government bias in the way modern Africa is seen is altered. Without these changes little of consequence will happen at village level.

Such a message is controversial and the argumentation inevitably and deliberately provocative. It is a simple fact that a civil war does not provide the best environment for farming, but to state that truism is to stir a pot of resentment. It is far easier to see all of Africa's present problems as colonial in origin. Some would wish to ignore the fact that aid provided in the form of foreign currency sometimes drifts into the purchase of arms. It is harsh to remind people that there are more expatriate experts in Africa now than during the colonial period. To swipe at the road-building mania in Africa is for some like invoking the litany of horror stories that fuel the anti-aid lobby. But to ignore the need for genuine criticism of the aid programme is merely to help its opponents.

While it is true that in the eighteenth century, 20 per cent of the world's population lived in Africa and by the year 2000 it is likely to be less than 13 per cent, it is the distribution of population that has gone awry. In many African countries, people are alternatively crowded into overused lands and elsewhere spread too thin. In the next fifteen years, the total population in Africa is expected to increase proportionately more rapidly than in most parts of the world, and for this to happen without a secure farming base is very dangerous.

If these issues were to be deliberately ignored by concentrating only on international economics, the humanitarian message would be blunted. Worse, it would open up a credibility gap where experts would once more be talking to experts. Where solutions would once again be seen as beyond the reach of individuals and solely the responsibility of governments. Somehow we must ensure that famine remains on the conscience of us all as individuals and we do not merely pass this particular concern back to government. That is a recipe for continued inertia.

The British public bought more copies of the Brandt Report than any other country in the world. But for all that, the Report's impact has been marked by a public acquiescence in the persistent lowering of the official aid budget in real terms and the flaunting of all the most important of its recommendations.

It was left to individuals, shocked and stunned by seeing in their own sitting rooms children starve on the BBC films, to respond with magnificent generosity. It is that impulse of spontaneous concern that must now be retained and built on so that we do not allow the implications of this famine to be forgotten.

It is far more likely that the important message of the need to enfranchise the world poor through low-cost credit will appeal to individuals in the West. It is now they who must convince their governments. The individual moved by humanitarian concern is far more likely to sense that an approach based on self-help will provide the incentive and restore human dignity. That it represents a more hopeful and indeed more realistic strategy than relying solely on the bureaucrats of government and international institutions.

The description of the herder's associations with a $6000 loan used as revolving credit and with a $4500 cereal credit demonstrates that, like other business people, if they have the money to replace their animals which represent their capital, they can prevent their enterprise running down. All over Africa there is immense scope for such local credit to end the impoverishment of the small farmer. Top-down agricultural theories on their own are totally insufficient to overcome the present crisis.

The urban orientation of African governments, the dominance of the capital city, the lack of a critical press reporting on the state of the rural economy and the absence, sometimes, of democratic pressure all contribute to the present crisis. For the future development of Africa to succeed, these factors must change as well. No strategy to eradicate famine can ignore them. We must think afresh and be far readier to challenge the conventional wisdoms. If this report fuels the debate, restores a sense of realistic hope and revives a mood of 'can do' optimism, then it will have made the contribution those of us associated with it hope for.

David Owen

Introduction

The root causes of the tragic situation now prevailing in many parts of Africa are multiple and complex. Simplification can be hazardous. To take sides in the debate on whether famine is a natural or a man-made disaster is unnecessary as well as undesirable. Of course, both elements are inextricably present. The question mark in the title of this book is, therefore, of particular significance.

We believe that if humanitarianism were to become a factor to reckon with in international relations, just as economic, political and security considerations are, this planet would be a better place to live in. The Independent Commission, which we have the honour to co-chair, was established because of the need to strengthen the human dimension in the global policy-making process. Our effort is directed to a hard-nosed review of the human condition. We plead for a voice, a decisive voice, for the mute multitudes – those hundreds of millions in all parts of the world who are destitute, vulnerable, unprotected.

Because a Commission dealing with humanitarian issues can only be concerned with what is essentially human, its research, analyses and deliberations must, of necessity, carry a clear emphasis, even at the expense of seeming to neglect other disciplines or aspects. Consequently, when in our plenary meetings we discussed the bleak scenario unfolding in Africa, we dealt more with the human tragedy than the global economic and political issues which contribute to it. We are aware that world recession, depressed commodity prices, problems of national debts and interest rates, unfavourable terms of trade and the high cost of energy are all factors directly relevant to the African situation and the acute food shortages leading to famine. Our research and reflection have, however, revolved around the human factor; mainly the rural poor who form the important but relatively neglected majority of African populations.

This book, which is based principally on the research and deliberations of the Commission, carries the same emphasis. Its purpose is to stress the humanitarian dimension in the current public debate and to facilitate further discussion by those concerned, including members of the Commission themselves.

It is our considered opinion that what is happening in Africa today can very well happen in other parts of the globe tomorrow. As forests retreat and deserts advance, as threats to essential life-support systems increase and ecological fragility grows, so will the vulnerability of the human race. If man continues in the profligate use of resources and to struggle against nature instead of co-operating with it to improve the quality of life, no continent may be spared the kind of problems now facing Africa, even though they may vary in scope and scale from region to region.

In any crisis of this kind, the highest price is always paid by the poorest. It is incumbent upon our common humanity to make their concerns our own and to help them as best we can. The privileged few and the very few need to be reminded that the poor and the very poor have legitimate aspirations to a better life on earth.

This book attempts a mixture of diagnosis and

prescription. It must be recognized though that there are no miraculous solutions and no shortcuts to the resolution of long-term problems. However, such a crisis is a time of opportunity as well as danger.

The situation in Africa is a challenge to man's ingenuity and instinct to survive. It is also a call on human compassion.

The destitute have a right to food which must not be denied by policy makers in the name of so-called economic realism. Policies devoid of humanitarian concerns lead not only to civil disturbances in urban areas but also, and above all, death and desolation in the countryside. They bring in their wake massive migrations of populations. We believe that, in terms of humanitarian assistance, what is perceived today as a moral imperative may tomorrow become a political necessity.

Solutions cannot be found just in offices and laboratories. They must be arrived at through a constant dialogue and interaction between those who are too often considered as objects of development and those who are in charge of development. The latter need not only humanitarian commitment and political will but also humility in dealing with complexity: our humanitarian plea is also a plea to recognize people's creativity. Illiteracy does not mean ignorance any more than knowledge means wisdom.

Innovative technical solutions appropriate to local or national circumstances require risk capital which present financial and credit systems hesitate to provide. Both relief aid and the credit systems should be geared to the needs and the wishes of farmers and herders in Africa. Donor and recipient governments must trust their capacity and help them help themselves on the difficult path to self-sufficiency.

The purpose of this book is not to apportion blame but to suggest alternative perceptions and solutions. It seeks to sow some 'seeds of hope' so that the harvest may benefit not only those struck by famine but also all those who are struggling to ensure for themselves and their children a life of self-reliance and dignity.

We feel that donors as well as recipients need to review their priorities as well as policies and practices governing aid to the rural poor. This goes also for the international financial systems including the World Bank and the International Monetary Fund. We need hardly emphasize that the real answer to Africa's problem is long-term economic and social development enabling it to become self-sufficient. However, looking into those aspects as thoroughly as they deserve to be examined is beyond the scope of this book. We are certain, though, that Africa needs in the years to come, more than ever before, a massive aid input from external sources, essentially to small farmers. We urge donors to provide it. The more it is timely and appropriate, the greater its impact.

Much is made of the role of media and particularly television in sensitizing public opinion to contemporary problems. However, all it requires is to press a button to move our attention from the horror of dying millions to the antic story of a prosperous 'Dynasty' whose main problem is its affluence. The paradox of our time is: if we can get to the moon and try to conquer space, can we allow millions of our fellow human beings to perish just because food, which is abundantly available elsewhere, could not be got to them in time?

Seldom before in human history has the need for a strategy to survive been so great; or man's ability to formulate one put so acutely to the test. Compassion and understanding and all those human ties which bind mankind together must rise to the challenge posed by Africa. This book is not a cry of anguish; it is a message of hope as well as an appeal for greater help to our fellow human beings in distress. Armed with faith in our common destiny we cannot, shall not, fail them.

Co-Chairmen: Hassan bin Talal   Sadruddin Aga Khan

Editorial note

This report is a part of the on-going process of research and reflection by the Independent Commission on International Humanitarian Issues relating to the tragic situation prevailing in many parts of Africa due to widespread famine.

It is a modest attempt to elaborate on the Commission's humanitarian message in a way which would allow it to be widely shared. A special effort was made to avoid making the report cumbersome reading. Hence, the absence of footnotes and detailed technical explanations. It is presented to the general public in the hope that it will increase awareness of the problems facing Africa in the context of famine and facilitate further study and analysis of the situation. Above all, it is intended to encourage the search for solutions as well as a greater effort by donors and recipients of humanitarian aid.

The report is based principally on deliberations of the Commission and the research done for it. It takes up the views expressed in the communiqués issued at the end of the two Plenary Meetings of the Commission in 1984, held in Tunisia and the Netherlands. The texts of these statements are included as an appendix to this book.

Research on specific aspects that this report deals with, such as systems of famine prediction, desertification, deforestation, etc., was carried out for the Independent Commission by G. Campbell; P. Cutler, C. Hogg,

J. Rivers, and F. D'Souza; B. Clark and L. Timberlake; D. Burn, R. van der Giesen and D. Poore.

Special input on various aspects of the report was brought by an expert group meeting, which was held at Nyon, Switzerland, in March 1985, attended notably by E. Bernus, O. Bremaud, M. Didier-Laurent, J. Derclayes, L. Filippi-Wilhelm, D. Kintz, E. Kane, and F. Vincent. It was preceded and followed by an extensive internal review of the text by the Secretariat of the Commission to which Pierre Spitz and Pablo Bifani in particular contributed. At the end of the process of technical review a group of the members of the Independent Commission met in Geneva in the framework of its Working Group on Disasters, to finalize comments on the draft. In addition, written comments on the draft were received from a number of the Commission members as well as experts. These helped improve the text in style and substance.

Special thanks are due to Mark Malloch Brown whose enthusiasm and ability contributed so much to the preparation of the book.

The technical preparation of the report was greatly facilited by the dedicated work of B. Balmer, P. Bond, J. Mico, M. de Sousa, A. Toh and D. Topali. The maps and diagrams were drawn by R. Natkiel and his associates.

Last, but not least, we wish to express our appreciation to David Kewley and his colleagues at Pan Books for their valuable support in the publication of this report.

Although a bibliography is not provided, the report's debt to writers such as Robert Chambers and Amartya Sen, the publications of the United Nations System including the World Bank, as well as many others will be apparent to those who are familiar with the literature.

Any income from sales of this book will be devoted entirely to research on humanitarian issues.

H. Beer   Z. Rizvi
Convenor   Secretary General
ICIHI Working Group on Disasters   ICIHI

                                        Geneva, April 1985

1 The famine

'Dawn, and as the sun breaks through the piercing chill of night on the plain outside Korem, it lights up a biblical famine, now, in the twentieth century. This place, say workers here, is the closest thing to hell on earth.' There had been famine in Ethiopia since at least 1983, but it was this BBC television broadcast, in October 1984, which is generally credited with having broken through the veil of ignorance.

Yet the famine was no secret. African governments had been doing their best to whip up international concern and there had been countless newspaper articles, television programmes and radio broadcasts about it. But whatever the individual impact of such pieces they were not to force a major international response until these strange haunting words with the graphic pictures of passive famine victims were flashed across the world. By that point there were serious food shortages in twenty African countries and millions of lives were at risk. Many had already been lost. For some African countries, international attention only came when the worst of the crisis was already over. (Throughout, we use the term Africa to refer to sub-Saharan Africa unless otherwise specified.)

This report is partly about how such a tragedy could have gone 'undiscovered' for so long. It seeks to establish why

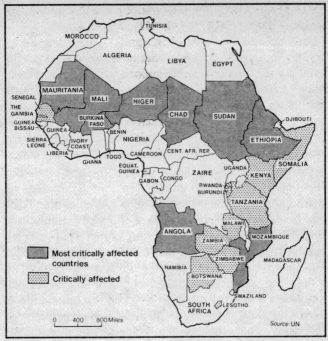

Map I

nothing happened until television alerted the world to a, by then, old disaster.

At each stage, from its genesis in rural poverty and food-production failures through to the reduction of communities to destitution and starvation, famine is avoidable. More than that, its causes are much more complex than just bad luck with the weather. The simple assumption that, if the rains fail, as they have in recent years in much of Africa, less food will be grown and people will inevitably starve, may be a comfortable abdication of any human responsibility for what has happened. But it is a misleading simplification. At each stage of the slow-burning fuse that can lead to famine other factors have fanned the flames.

Famine is that moment when a group's normal access to food so completely collapses that mass starvation occurs. But it is wrong to leave the definition at that. Famine is also characterized by widespread disruption as people migrate or in other ways radically break with normal behaviour in their search for food. A lot of statistics have been thrown around about the number of people affected by the famine. Statistics are a handy tool much too lightly used to dramatize tragic situations; their variety and vagueness undermine.

Most Africans have an inadequate diet at the best of times. Famine conditions rarely occur in a country as a whole but in particular localities. By early 1985 the United Nations had refined its estimates of the numbers seriously affected by food shortages and in urgent need of food aid to 30 million.

A further indication of the precise scope of the disaster is the calculation that it has created up to 10 million migrants. Elsewhere, governments have the means to avert such migrations with the political and social consequences they bring with them but not in Africa. In all the countries that map I shows as being seriously affected by famine, there have been very large movements of people. These have either been within countries or, increasingly, across national borders, for example, from Ethiopia and Chad into Sudan, from Niger into Nigeria and so on.

Famine then is more than people dying from starvation. It is an acute breakdown of society that brings turmoil that cannot be ignored. This can take different forms: the listless passive victims in the Ethiopian relief camps probably were, as it happened, more effective in generating action than say, bread riots would have been. A major famine-relief operation in Sudan had already begun on the tail of the Ethiopian famine before the bread riots in Khartoum in April 1985. But whether protesting or reduced to listlessness by hunger, famine victims are a threat to stability. This differentiates famine from the endemic life-threatening hunger that is the permanent lot of many Africans. At the time of the last major African famine in the early 1970s, it was thought that chronic hunger and malnutrition were the regular condition of eighty million Africans. That number is now 100 million. Each year the rate of growth of the population exceeds that of food production. The permanent food crisis therefore worsens year by year.

So famine is the tip of a much bigger underlying crisis. Even when Ethiopia is free of famine, 1000 children are thought to die each day of malnutrition and related illnesses. What distinguishes famine from starvation and run-of-the-mill food shortages, however severe, is that famine is political. In desperation starving people flee their homes and by doing so they drop their problem into someone else's lap, either their own government or the neighbouring government and the international community. There are currently large numbers of destitute migrants, famine victims, on the outskirts of many of the towns and cities of the affected African countries.

It need not be like that. For example, in parts of Asia with potential famine risk, villagers are usually able to muster enough public influence to get government assistance before they are forced to migrate in search of food. Obviously, that is a much more satisfactory state of affairs than leaving help until later when people are destitute and far from home. But at whatever stage outside aid comes, the crucial factor is that the victims have exhausted their own means of coping and outsiders, be they the local authorities, the national government or foreign donors feel obliged to intervene and do something about it.

The victims of the present famine in Africa are the rural poor. Almost without exception they are people who are powerless. Many live outside the normal reach of government services. Among the countries which have been worst hit, there have been large numbers of people living on the edge of the Sahara desert where often the only viable agriculture is nomadic livestock raising. Even at the best of times there may not be enough water for crops. Nomads, particularly, have little regular access to schools, health clinics and other services, let alone the opportunity to organize themselves as a force to reckon with. Peasant farmers are often little better off.

Ironically, only the ultimate crisis of destitution, famine, has brought these people a voice, and even then not an organized one. But in their distress they suddenly pose a threat to governmental structures and are at last able to impose themselves on the conscience of others. In that latter aspect the power of the media, especially television, has been crucial.

Famine, as a word, carries with it the implication that the user means to do something about it: bring help; criticize others for not doing enough; contribute to a charity collection; but certainly in some way to act. It is an acknowledgement that fellow human beings have reached that stage of utter despair where we must help.

This report looks at how the crisis of African rural life can be brought into view so that the symptoms of famine can be detected at an early stage and treated before there is massive destitution or loss of life. Although earlier relief assistance can limit the human costs, the more important ambition must be to help communities to restore the economic viability of rural life and so reduce the risk of famine. For both purposes, we are persuaded that, because famine is the visible dimension of a long-standing crisis of Africa's rural poor, what is essential is that policies be pursued which economically and politically re-enfranchise this group and so address the underlying causes. Farmers' traditional capacity to cope with routine setbacks of weather must be restored and strengthened.

An emphasis on the rural sector is now the established wisdom of both governments and the international aid community. In the chapters that follow we show how this process has been, despite good intentions, counterproductive. If Africa is not to stumble from one famine to another with increasing frequency, the rural poor must be put first. In some countries, this understanding is being translated into reality. Throughout, policies made for urban people by urban people have pushed aside the needs of the rural majority. Food prices have been kept artificially low to benefit urban consumers rather than rural producers. Investment, education and welfare have gone to the towns first. The crisis is one not just of neglect but also policy errors. When policies have touched on the countryside they have often demonstrated doubtful priorities. For example, when there have been price incentives for producers often they have been for cash crops rather than local foods. Irrigation schemes have overlooked overall water shortage and the farming practices of the area. Aid projects have often encouraged nomads to give up their old lives and settle down in a way the land cannot support. The list is depressingly long.

The consequence is that far from the dramatic spotlight of famine, the quality of rural life as a whole is deteriorating dangerously. The loss of forests means that each year people are having to go further and further in search of firewood; women are spending an even larger number of working hours carrying water from distant sources; live-stock owners have to migrate ever further in search of grazing land; cultivators are forced to leave shorter and shorter fallow periods before re-using land.

It is easy to dismiss comparisons between Africa and, say, India or China. The soils of the Asian countries are generally richer. Nevertheless the contrasting agricultural performance gives some measure of how badly wrong things have gone in Africa. India, population about 740 million, has a land area only a third larger than Sudan, population 21 million. India feeds itself. This year Sudan will not; and many of its neighbours have lost all fore-seeable prospect of feeding themselves again.

The pages that follow offer hope to those who fear an endless African dependence on external aid. Criticism of what has gone wrong carries with it the assumption that things can equally well be put right. Recovery does not rest only on luck or the weather but also on good organization in the broadest sense. Those African governments which are trying to redress the situation must be actively encouraged and helped to do so.

There is a need to make a balanced assessment of how the African crisis arose, not in order to assign blame but to suggest alternatives to whatever failures of policy have occurred. It is not enough to debate to what extent the disaster is natural or man-made. It is equally important to bear in mind the inhospitable international environment as well as domestic economic conditions. That some in Africa have used the weather as an excuse to cover failures of policy does not invalidate the enormous difficulties under which African agriculture operates. There is a degree of variability of rainfall not experienced in temperate zones. In some semi-arid areas rain has not fallen for years. African farmers, especially those in such areas, have always existed in a precarious balance with their harsh environment. In recent years, this balance has been disturbed. The land has been unable to meet the demands put upon it and has degenerated. Instead of nature producing its own harsh correctives to the cycle of drought and rainfall, an ecological and human disaster has engulfed parts of Africa.

Superimposed on the harsh rigours of climate has been an equally unfavourable international economic environment. This has been described elsewhere, notably in the two reports of the Independent Commission on International Development Issues (the Brandt reports) and in statements of African leaders, such as the Lagos Plan of Action. We do not propose to reiterate their conclusions here at great length, though they need to be kept clearly in view.

Most African economies are small in international terms and highly specialized, usually exporting one or two primary commodities – a legacy of colonial times, despite some progress in diversification. Such economies are highly vulnerable to the vagaries of international trade. External shocks – such as large swings in commodity prices, or the big increase in the price of oil – affect not only exporters themselves but have a major impact on the balance of payments, government budgets and private investment.

These economies are subject not only to internationally induced instability. Many commodity exporters have suffered a prolonged deterioration in their terms of trade. Over the last ten years, African countries have lost as much as 20 per cent of the purchasing power of their exports. Even as the world economy seemed to be turning the corner in 1984, the recovery seemed to pass Africa by, and commodity prices, in dollar terms, fell. One contributory factor has been the desperate need of many developing countries – in Latin America as well as Africa – to improve their external imbalance by exporting larger volumes to the world market, thus depressing prices.

Africa has also been unable to mobilize adequate capital externally to transform its productive potential. As living standards have fallen, so inevitably have domestic savings. As a share of gross domestic product (GDP), savings in low-income Africa fell from 13.4 per cent in 1970 to 5.9 per cent in 1981. External capital is therefore even more urgently required than a decade ago. Yet capital flows in the form of aid have stagnated. Attempts by African countries to borrow their way out of stagnation have led to debt-service payments rising to over 25 per cent in 1983 from 8.8 per cent a decade earlier. As a consequence, African countries have accounted for half of all debt reschedulings experienced in recent years and a good many others are in arrears on debt service. Projections by the International Monetary Fund (IMF) suggest that even on relatively favourable assumptions about world growth and interest rates, the burden of debt service will get worse. And the generally optimistic World Bank has shown that even modest improvements in debt-servicing ratios will be at the price of another decade of falling per-capita incomes. The combination of smaller loan inflows and higher interest payments means that the net transfer from the rich world to Africa slumped by more than 50 per cent between 1980 and 1983. The World Bank estimates that an additional $6 billion is required per year to keep net flows at the far from generous levels of 1980–82.

This economic crisis has had a direct bearing on the food crisis. Because of the shortage of foreign exchange, factories can no longer operate and supply spare parts needed for farm equipment or consumer goods for peasant farmers to buy. Because of petrol shortages and budget cuts, farm extension workers do not get into the field and

31

there is a deterioration in the quality of transport to and from the countryside. Ports, airports and telephone systems deteriorate below the level reached to handle an emergency. Because of the need, impressed on governments by the IMF, to give overriding priority to short-run financial stabilization, long-term development and reconstruction plans have to be postponed, cut or abandoned; and priority has to be given to those sectors of farming which generate the most foreign exchange, rather than food for local consumption.

The absence of further detailed attention to these issues in the report in no sense implies any lack of recognition of their enormous importance and of the need for a radically improved external environment and greater assistance. We shall, however, concentrate on ways in which international assistance and national policy can be reorientated to restore the primacy of small-scale farming. Moreover, where we do make criticisms we stress that these must be balanced against the international economic factors. Real incomes are falling in Africa and there is no short term prospect of that changing. In many cases, the majority of declining government revenues is now inevitably taken up in paying salaries and other recurrent costs; there is virtually nothing left for investment in development of any kind. Without external assistance, African governments do not have the means to bring about a major shift of resources from city to countryside. The resources are just not there and national stability will not allow for further cuts in urban living standards. Therefore, the resources for a new rural initiative must come principally from outside the continent, from the aid donors. The attraction is that the sums of money needed to help the rural sector find its feet are not impossibly large. Combined with firm leadership from African governments, it offers a path back from the development follies of the past to a sustainable small-scale approach that would enjoy much greater support.

What the present famine has done is help create the intellectual climate for such a re-think. A frank and self-critical appraisal of 'development' efforts has already begun. It is widely accepted that wrong paths to growth have been followed. Too often 'white elephants' which are inappropriate for Africa's needs have been put up; what Edgard Pisani, the former EEC commissioner for development, dismissed as cathedrals in the desert. As a reading of the Lagos Plan of Action shows, governments have been as frank as anybody in acknowledging mistakes. In 1984, at least ten African governments announced plans to devolve agricultural responsibilities, particularly for marketing, to the village or farmer associations. At least, sixteen governments have either raised the price of farm products or removed price controls altogether. This is a necessary but modest beginning.

Too many aid donors have slipped into the 'we know best' approach. For donor governments it may be a relief to escape the seemingly interminable public inquiries that precede so many construction projects back home. In the Third World the opposite prevails. If an aid donor and a government minister reach an understanding on a project, be it a hydro-electric dam that displaces thousands of people or a road that cuts through forest lands, there are few, if any, legal or political constraints. Africa has too frequently been a laboratory for the fancies of foreign development experts.

Intertwined with the crisis of the rural economy in Africa is a crisis of government itself. One reflection of this is the urban bias in policy-making and the absence of rural participation. Governments have been preoccupied with the needs of the new, and economically under-productive,

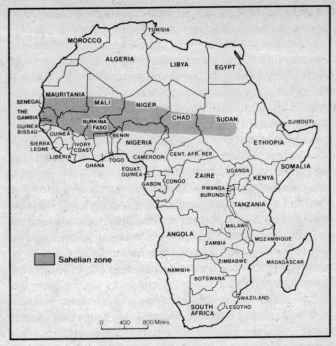

Map II

cities. Indeed, catering to the aspirations of the urbanites has sometimes been a prerequisite for politcal survival.

The price has been paid in the countryside. Other aspects of the difficulties post-colonial governments have had in establishing their authority have also played their part. In five of the worst-affected countries, Angola, Chad, Ethiopia, Mozambique and Sudan, famine co-exists beside internal disturbances and armed conflicts directed against the central government. Across Africa, scarce resources have been pulled away from investment in development, in order to give priority to maintaining the authority of central governments. This includes arms spending.

The strain on governments can only grow as the famine-induced migration gathers pace. Even as the geographical reach of the famine has lessened, it appears to have intensified in the Sahel belt of states across Africa (see map II), and its tentacles still stretch firmly into Sudan and Ethiopia. In these countries, life has become increasingly unsupportable on the desert frontline. Famine and the encroaching desert have brought about irreversible changes in the demographic map of the continent.

In the second half of the book we turn to how the African economy could be managed in the interests of rural development so as to overcome the gulf between cities and the countryside. We look at the need to restore an agriculture whose income-generating benefits reach the poorest and which lives within its environmental means. We also propose how international assistance can be remodelled to support these goals.

However, the famine reflects so deep a crisis that it would be unrealistic to believe that even radical policy changes could avert further major food breakdowns in the short-term. Therefore, the mechanisms to avert, or at least contain, famine must be improved. This is the subject of the next two chapters.

2 Before disaster

People only see what they are prepared to see.

Emerson, 1839

Famine should not be a surprise. It is the culmination of a series of crises, each of which has set off its own alarm signals. Yet disaster assistance nearly always comes too late. There is still no adequate early warning system of impending disaster.

The circumstances which lead to famine actually build up quite slowly. Unlike an earthquake which strikes suddenly, famine occurs after one, or probably more, years of food supply difficulties. So there are obvious advantages in trying to forecast it, and on the face of it no reasons why this should be a difficult exercise. Yet attempts to do so in Africa have been repeatedly confounded. The best known early warning system is run by the UN Food and Agriculture Organization (FAO). Data is collected about rainfall; if the rain does not come at the right time, or fails altogether it is a signal that a lot of the seed will not germinate. Also, estimates are made of what acreage has been planted and then, at harvest time, further calculations are completed of how much has been grown. So it would seem that FAO should, together with the governments who help it collect this material, be well-placed to sound the alarm if at any stage its monitoring indicates that something is going wrong. The record tells a different story.

The Ethiopian government, after the 1972 to 1974 famine, instituted the most complete early warning system of its kind in Africa. Local officials are supposed to monitor rainfall, crop planting and harvests and then regularly turn in their data to a small unit in the government's Relief and Rehabilitation Commission (RRC). This unit collates the information and provides a series of crop estimates throughout the year as each stage of the planting and harvesting cycle is completed. On the basis of these estimates, the RRC has warned the donors of a prospective food crisis every year for the last eleven years – each year of its existence.

Although it is true that population growth, misinvestment in state farms, soil deterioration and the civil war in the north have made Ethiopia endemically short of food, annual warnings of famine are rather too like the little boy who cries wolf once too often. The warnings were not believed. The system seems to lack credibility with donors.

Institutionally, although held up as a model of its kind, it is unclear whether the small unit responsible for collating the information inside the RRC has had the clout to ensure that the local officials give enough attention to collecting precise data. Additionally, collection of rainfall statistics is only useful if there are sufficient collection stations under disciplined management.

Some of the driest areas of northern Ethiopia are ones which government officials can often not reach, hence further weakening the data collection. The next step, calculating the shortfall between needs and the prospective harvest, is less reliable still. The RRC unit in Addis Ababa attempts to arrive at a calculation of national deficit. But until late 1984, the government and donors were formally operating under the assumption that there were nine million fewer Ethiopians than there are now believed to be. A new census upped the population in 1984 but if the old calculations of harvest size and food requirement had borne any relation to reality, these nine million people would have remained neglected. But once the new census findings were known, the calculation of how many food rations were needed was not suddenly raised. Everybody, government, international agencies and others, accepts the imprecision of the method and guess as best they can what the approximate truth is. Hardly a process to reinforce the confidence of food donors.

One of the weaknesses of the weather and crop yield based system of early warning is that, although information is collected locally, the calculation of shortage is made on a national basis. For some years there have been intensifying shortages, localized famines, in northern Ethiopia. These have, to some extent, been offset by surpluses elsewhere in the country. It is rare for famine to take a whole country in its grip. Yet these crucial regional differences are blunted in the national statistics. An inter-governmental early warning system, which is what the FAO one is, is conditioned by its reliance on national governments for information. Sometimes, such information may have, or be perceived by donors to have, a partial character.

At present in some African countries famine conditions cover much of the country, but this is the exception rather than the rule of famine. More typically famines are highly localized. Famine only spread to the southern part of Ethiopia in 1984. Equally, in Sudan, there has been increasingly serious malnutrition in the west for some years and also patches in the east in the Red Sea Province. But it was the failure of the harvest in the normally surplus producing regions of central and eastern Sudan that tipped the country as a whole into famine in 1985.

Monitoring food shortage requires a much closer focus on the local anatomy of famine. In Africa, the inefficient road and transport system and weak market mechanisms often mean that if a particular area suffers a deficit in the midst of its neighbours' surplus, people will go hungry. Without outside intervention food will not move from surplus to deficit areas. But in national calculations of food shortage, the implications of these crucial local differences do not show up. Nor is climate a guide to whether there are social and economic constraints on food moving within a country from the surplus to the deficit regions. The price mechanism (people will be prepared to pay more for food if their locality is short of it) should draw supplies into the deficit area. But will the people who need food still have money to buy it?

Even if they do, the market mechanisms may be too underdeveloped for that demand to make the link with surplus supplies elsewhere. Perhaps the two areas have no tradition of trade between each other. Or alternatively, those with a surplus may view their neighbour's deficit as a warning of what may come to them the following year and therefore store the food rather than sell it. Perhaps those in the deficit area did, in fact, store food themselves the previous year, so that they can cope to some extent with a harvest failure – in which case, their need in the first year of harvest failure may not be as great as the raw data of crop yield might suggest.

Measuring the weather and crop size will obviously not answer many of these crucial questions. But answers to them are vital in deciding what drought will mean for a particular area. Hence, social scientists have provided an alternative model of famine early warning based on people's behaviour. If there is panic, it is a sure sign that food is not reaching deficit areas at a price vulnerable people can afford. Such evidence of imminent crisis may not come as early as measuring the rainfall, but it is much surer evidence that local communities have failed to cope with the setback of bad weather, and it is a much better indication that outside help, either from the national or international level, is required.

Such signals of social and economic distress have the same seasonal pattern to them as the weather-based indicators. Food shortage in the countryside is not constant throughout the year but is tied to the farming cycle. In a normal year, the worst months will be those immediately preceding the harvest. Last year's food stocks will have run down and there may only be just enough food to eke out the weeks until the harvest. At this point the farmer may well be having to buy food. If the harvest then fails, people may be well down the road to acute food shortage. Although a harvest, however poor, will have improved their position from a month earlier, food shortage will soon be much more acute than it was at the same point a year before.

The essential point is that country life is potentially rich with signals of crisis, but these are seasonal. The observer, with an urban experience, has little sensitivity to this time-dimension of food supply. In the cities, the availability of food is largely governed by arbitrary commercial factors rather than the seasons.

Basing famine forecasting on human rather than crop behaviour is not new. The most famous example is the famine code instituted in India by the British in the nineteenth century. District officers were expected to be on the lookout for any growth in the crime rate which could be attributed to food shortage, any increase in the number of destitute migrants, or any rise in the number of starvation-related deaths. Prior to these advanced social signs of impending localized famine, the market price for food already begins to behave erratically. Broadly, grain prices will rise sharply, independent of any normal seasonal fluctuations and livestock prices will plummet as people sell precious animals to buy food grain for their own consumption. If the reason for food shortage is drought, this will give further impetus to the forced sale of livestock at give-away prices.

To the observer in the right place, looking for the right signs, an imminent famine becomes hard to miss. The Independent Commission on International Humanitarian Issues (ICIHI) has financed research by the London-based Food Emergencies Research Unit (FERU) to carry out field research in various parts of Africa in order to collect basic data and verify the conceptual foundations of such a system. An attempt was then to be made to see whether it is possible to establish a continent-wide network of voluntary groups to monitor such socio-economic signals and warn when shortages are imminent. This project is being supported by ICIHI in the hope that this addition to the existing early warning system would lead to more reliable indicators of impending disasters. The monitoring system would be based on a series of agreed indicators concerning the behaviour of market prices for food at the local level, and signs of panic such as people selling household goods or being forced to migrate. All are signals of a localized food crisis.

In other words, the behaviour of potential famine victims is the least fallible guide to the onset of famine. Food donors would then be presented with early warning data which would accurately pinpoint communities unable to cope. Obviously, it would be a great improvement on the present national estimates with their improbable assumptions about population size, national crop area and likely yields.

Because weather-based systems have such a poor track record, social scientists are inclined to discount altogether weather and crop yields as indicators. This may be going too far the other way, particularly now that satellites allow much better crop surveys than was previously the case, offering a broad guide to where crop failure is likely. Although they are no substitute for local level socio-economic research, the searchers on the ground can get a better idea where to look. At present there is a risk that different early warning systems will remain jealously guarded rival preserves of single academic disciplines. It would be much better if the social scientists, the meteorologists and the agronomists joined forces.

However, even a successful partnership of satellite photography and social scientist *in situ* may not be enough to make donors commit food aid when warned that a famine is just round the corner. Committing emergency aid prior to visible starvation requires more than technocratic judgement; it also needs political courage. Those who have been quick to criticize Western and other governments for not foreseeing the African famine and delivering food in time would have been as angry if food aid had been delivered when it was not needed. Not only would it have been a waste of public funds, but the arrival of large amounts of free food, surplus to the recipient country's requirements, would have forced local food prices down. This, in turn, could trigger food shortages the following year by discouraging local farmers from growing a surplus. Prices would have become so low due to the glut of food aid on the market that it would no longer be worth the local farmer's while to grow a surplus for sale. Even with huge surpluses in the North, there are plenty of reasons why cautious officials will resist shipping food.

There is no better spur to tangible action than beaming starving people in the South via television into the living-rooms of the North. But it is a sad and belated way of making the point.

It is suggested that the reason there has not been a major famine in India since 1943 is not just because of the improved food production, but also because it has a free press functioning in a democratic framework. If an area within the country starts to slip towards crisis, victims can make their voice heard. Newspapers kick up a fuss, thus stirring the concern of the central authorities. Hence timely action. In Africa, regrettably, there is rarely the same link between countryside and urban politicians. In general, there is a lack of representative structures which allow rural voices to be heard. During the present famine, many of those in other continents who have seen starving people on television have been closer than many in Africa to what is happening.

The world community needs to be sensitized on the food issue. There is enough food in the world to feed everybody and barriers should not be erected to prevent emergency distribution of food when required. Hence the obligation to develop an early warning system which is trusted. If the food is available to prevent famine it should be given in time. The argument about how that food is provided so that it does not exacerbate the problems of local food production is a separate issue that we will deal with later. Here, we wish to stress that society as a whole must come to accept the concept of an international humanitarian food-flow until countries have secured their own self-sufficiency in food production. Governments in food-deficit countries must overcome their disinclination to ask for outside help. Lives must not be lost because of national pride or a lack of foresight.

The Ethiopian government had certainly been sounding the alarm internationally for over a year before a television team suddenly brought the crisis alive and galvanized international action in October 1984. But the government had not come clean with its own people about the famine. It had not undertaken the belt-tightening measures, such as cutting back on arms purchases or foregoing the expensive celebrations of the revolution, which a government with real accountability to those in the countryside might have been obliged to do. Only a much more unequivocal clearing of the decks on its part to fight famine at the expense of other government priorities might have persuaded sceptical food donors to act sooner.

Although the European Economic Community (EEC) had a major food aid programme in Ethiopia, Western governments for the most part kept their distance. There was little to prompt them to send food to Ethiopia in preference to other hungry African countries, or indeed in preference to keeping it in storage in Europe and Northern America. This was not least because of the Ethiopian dependence on the Soviet Union and its allies for aid.

Overnight, public opinion provided a compelling reason to help Ethiopia. In Sudan, the government for different reasons delayed an international response to the famine. Again, more representative political structures would not have allowed it to do so. It would seem that national pride about throwing itself on the mercy of the international community coupled with concern that panic-talk of shortages would encourage powerful grain merchants to corner supplies, and a failure to appreciate the extent of some of the local shortages led the Sudanese government to hold back from a general appeal for international help. Whatever the justification for this approach, if the mute voice of the famine victims had been heard, the government would have reacted sooner. As it was, response on any scale only took place when famine victims trekked to Omdurman and other towns along the Nile. Effectively they were bringing their case to the government's own doorstep.

A credible network of voluntary groups might help alert

governments in the international community to impending trouble. It would, however, be unrealistic to believe that it would make a big difference without a much clearer international commitment to a human right to food in a world which has a surplus. Regrettably at present, the victims only gain power and the ear of those with food to spare when their plight becomes so acute that through the media or through their appearance on the streets of the capital, they become an issue for those in power. Their disaster is ironically the source of their temporary ascendancy. Pre-empting famine would also mean pre-empting the constellation of forces that girds governments into helping the victims.

Voluntary agencies' importance in famine prevention lies in the confidence they often enjoy at several very different levels. At each, the basis for the trust put in them is their non-governmental character. At the international level their findings about a local situation of food shortage are trusted. They are thought not to have an axe to grind. Similarly at the local level, they may be a more accepted source of intervention and advice for the victims. They are crucial actors in building up the sense of global 'community' in dealing with famine and a human right to food.

So is the press. Yet journalists have had immense difficulties getting access to a number of the famine-affected areas. Governments, in general, do not like foreign media. Sometimes they are no more keen on their own national press. There is little tolerance of criticism. Of course, arguments can fairly be made about the imbalance of world news. But the obstacles placed in the way of the media reporting the African famine cannot be attributed to that. Here was the Western media for once pursuing with all its commercial zest an African story.

Once the African famine made the front page and the evening TV news bulletins, attitudes changed. Visas were showered on journalists like confetti, although one or two countries, as much because of transport shortage as any lingering wish to censor, still could not let in the journalists except as a trickle. So Mozambique's famine, for example, continued to be under-reported. But for the most part, Africa briefly acknowledged the power of the media.

If governments and the aid agencies are serious about quick response to future famines, the media must be brought in, and allowed to operate without censorship or restrictions on access. Only in such an environment will outside reporting about Africa improve and, more importantly, only then will the national press in Africa develop, and be able to become the poor man's advocate.

We have examined the limitations of conventional famine early warning systems, and showed why measuring the rain is not an accurate guide to how many poor people will be unable to buy food. In their place we have proposed a greater emphasis on socio-economic indicators of behaviour as people begin to foresee famine. We have described ICIHI's current inquiry into whether it would be feasible to establish an Africa-wide network of voluntary agencies to report on these indicators. It is part of our overall emphasis on reorientating government policy and aid structures so that they hear and see the small farmer. We have also argued that, however good the early warning system, it will require political will on the part of donors and recipients if food is to be shipped before famine reaches the television screens. In this regard we have stressed the need for recognition by society at large that all should have access to food. But averting famine remains a distant goal, therefore in the next chapter we look at the actions of governments and aid agencies after the onset of a disaster which was not prevented.

3 After disaster

Amid a multitude of projects, no plan is devised.

Publius Syrus, 1st century BC

An efficient system of famine prediction can provide more notice of impending disaster; however, the underlying fragility of Africa means that the international community, more particularly African communities themselves, must expect further breakdowns of the food supply. Community self-reliance should be the ambition, but for a long time the economic vulnerability of so many Africans to setbacks from the weather and other causes means that externally provided relief will have a role. As we write, nine of the twenty famine-affected countries in Africa, Angola, Burkina Faso, Chad, Ethiopia, Mali, Mauritania, Mozambique, Niger and Sudan required the essential life-support systems of major international relief operations. Without such interventions millions of lives were at risk. Eleven other countries also required extra food and other more limited types of assistance.

Relief has traditionally been seen as a stop-gap to give communities time while they recover after a disaster. Its short-term goals make it fundamentally different from development assistance. Development reduces the risk of disaster by alleviating poverty. But for a long time relief, in the classic sense, was not seen as doing more than putting the damage right after a disaster. It had no aspirations to forge long-term change.

So while relief is a matter of food, blankets, medical care and other temporary help to bridge the period during which people cannot help themselves, development aid is such things as farms, clinics, roads, schools and the services which go with them.

Many agencies, which do not have a clear mandate to work either solely in relief or in development, have agonized over how to divide their energies between the two. In rural communities as far apart as Burkina Faso and Vietnam, variations of a proverb which make this point can be found: give a man a fish and you feed him for a day; give him a fishing net and you feed him for life.

The inadequacy of early warning, coupled, in some cases, with a lack of political will to respond effectively until famine has burst in full force, means that essential time is lost for the phase which precedes full scale relief: containment.

The longer governments and the international community wait to respond the greater the irreversible damage and the cost. This is not only in lives lost but in the dislocation and separation of the victims from their means of livelihood. If no relief is forthcoming in their home villages, famine victims migrate. Once they have done so the economic, and sometimes the political, difficulties of reconnecting them to their former lives are multiplied.

At the containment stage, prompt action in their home areas can prevent the migration. We discuss later the political constraints on this. Here we would just note that the mandate and operations of the relief agencies militate against acting at this stage. Large inter-governmental agencies, frequently the only ones with the clout to be able to intervene at the village level before a famine is officially acknowledged, are often able to move only when the visible signs of famine provide the necessary pretext.

Pre-emptive action is politically more difficult than reactive ways of dealing with crisis. As we argue in the next chapter, food shortage turns to famine mainly because, in the absence of assistance, people lose the purchasing power to buy food.

An early intervention to restore that purchasing power by giving victims cash can avert widespread starvation. The United Nations Children's Fund (UNICEF), following the lead of a number of voluntary agencies, used such a pilot scheme to some effect in Ethiopia in 1984. It works because, as we argued in the last chapter, famine is usually localized. If the victims have money to spend, food will, in many instances, be drawn into the area where there is a shortage. But handing out money goes against the grain of relief assistance. Too many agencies still feel more comfortable with massive food aid operations. So the opportunity for more discreet, effective and earlier intervention is lost. Relief starts when the food trucks roll.

As long as relief is not linked to long-term development, thoughtful people will question its usefulness. Whereas the planning cycle of development projects can take years, with each step in implementation painstakingly prepared, relief by its very nature demands instant action and quick judgement. It is more visible but also more ephemeral. At best it is a band-aid. Or at least that is a popular estimate of it. In fact, despite a high profile, relief accounts for a small part of most donor governments' aid budgets.

But is the concept of relief as predominantly a band-aid an accurate one? Some think not. Agencies are starting to see relief, not just as a distraction from their main development work, but also as an opportunity. The Chinese word for disaster means both danger and opportunity. Disaster strikes at, and exposes the vulnerability of, those the aid agencies should most want to reach – the poorest. With the disruption of disaster, there is an opening to reach where it is ordinarily hard to get. Custom and hierarchy, often barriers between outside helpers and the most vulnerable, may be forced aside for the duration of a disaster.

The famine in Africa demonstrates another fact about disasters and their aftermath. Things do not return to where they were before. Relief operations, whatever they aspire to be, are not a patching up of the shattered past. The past is lost. A famine leaves lasting changes in the economic balance of power within society. It makes the poor poorer and the rich richer. Famines have often led to African herdsmen having to sell their livestock to absentee owners. As poor people sell at a low price everything they have in order to survive, somebody is getting richer.

Famine also changes the demographic map; it makes people move. So relief aid is an intervention in a situation of upheaval and intense change. The notion that it can somehow be neutral and bring about a return to the previous social configuration is wrong. Africa will not be the same as it was in 1983 when this round of famine is at an end. Wealth differentials will have increased and millions of people will have moved. Relief aid may mitigate some of the effects, but it will not restore the status quo.

Vast numbers of people, mostly illiterate, who have often lived outside the reach of government and modern services, are thrown into contact with, and dependence on, the outside world. Drought forces them to move, forsake old homes, meet new people, confront new choices. Ironically, in their misery, these people may land on the first rung of non-subsistence life. At the same time, their economic position, and capacity for self-sufficiency, become more marginal than ever. This is the context into which the relief worker steps. It is obviously one of opportunity and risk. The present structure of relief acknowledges little of this. The relief community seeks to be judged on the technocratic standard of its efficiency in delivering emergency supplies, not on its role as social engineer.

The main relief commodity is food. It is also the most difficult to handle both in the sense of transportation but also in its impact on those it is supposed to help. United Nations estimates of emergency food requirements in Africa have climbed ever higher during the famine. By March 1985 they were seven million tonnes. Taken together with commercial imports and non-emergency food aid (which in 1982 amounted to 9.25 million tonnes) it means that about two in every five Africans in the sub-Saharan countries are living on foreign food in 1985.

The experience of food aid, however, is that it creates a dependence on outside sources of food, both by changing tastes and by undermining the price of local food, thereby discouraging production. There is no doubt that it is a two-edged weapon and that it can very quickly contribute to the problem of hunger that it seeks to ameliorate. The danger that emergency food aid will be habit-forming is particularly great when the warehouses in the West are bursting with surplus food that government subsidies have encouraged farmers to grow. The food has to be put somewhere. The fortunate convergence of the opposite needs of donors and recipients could quickly become a permanent snare. Already as food aid is pumped in, the definition of emergency needs is becoming blurred. Too much food going into countries now recovering from famine will not assist recovery. Rather it may well retard it.

The food aid debate is not a new one. Briefly put, on the one side are those who argue that many developing countries are not presently growing enough to feed their populations and that therefore the provision of surplus Western food must reduce malnutrition. Because it is surplus to Western needs it will be provided, whereas extra money for the developing countries, which food-aid critics demand instead, would not be. So it allows a country to save precious foreign exchange which would otherwise have to be used to finance commercial food imports.

On the other side, the critics argue that it provides a respectable cover for dumping surplus food to keep prices high at home while making the recipient country's own food production uneconomic. How can a local producer compete against free foreign food?

In fact most food aid is usually not sold free. Rather the recipient government sells it and is expected to use the local currency funds that it earns from this for development work. As Western grains in surplus may not coincide with local tastes (for example, spare rice may initially appear a funny gift to a sorghum-eating African country), new tastes take hold.

As a consequence in dry countries, which have tended traditionally to grow sorghum and millet because they need less rain, the phenomenon emerges of city folk who develop an appetite for wheat or rice.

As countries get richer they get less food aid, but in many cases turn to importing food. In fact sub-Saharan Africa is the only region of the world where food aid per head has not been declining since the 1960s.

However, whatever the risks, food aid is clearly needed now in Africa. Distribution must be organized, keeping the dangers in mind and an eye on local market conditions. If there is local food available, the food aid must not be allowed to damage the farmer's price incentive to sell. In other circumstances where merchant-speculators are hoarding food in expectation of even higher prices, flooding the market with food aid to bring prices down can force merchants to sell. So an understanding of the particular market conditions with which food aid is interacting is vital.

Also food aid must be distributed as close as possible to the famine victims' homes. Hence our stress on right of access for relief operations. If, for political reasons, the food has to be distributed on the other side of a national border, it will become a magnet that draws people away from their homes and makes their rehabilitation more difficult. It may even turn them into refugees by default; stranded on the wrong side of a national border they never meant to cross.

From the first, food aid must be properly programmed. Where it is not being sold, it should be tied to well-structured food for work programmes. Food should be given in return for work on community projects designed to rehabilitate the agricultural sector and should be phased out as recovery takes place.

Finally, the food donors and African governments must be certain that famine has actually been brought about by a greater than usual food shortage.

As we show in chapter 4, famine occurs largely because of lack of purchasing power amongst the poor. A crop failure is the probable, although not inevitable, reason for this.

Beyond the question of food itself, relief managers are running up against Africa's decaying and inadequate infrastructure: ports without sufficient unloading capacity or warehousing; roads which have fallen into disrepair and bridges that are down; in many areas vehicles have to use little more than tracks without hard surfaces which, when the rains do finally come, will be impassable for heavy trucks; a shortage of lorries, spare parts and drivers; not

53

enough fuel; inadequate medical facilities and supplies; insufficient wells and other drinking water sources; and much more. The inadequacy of these basic essentials of a modern economy have held Africa back; and they now handicap the relief operation.

In such circumstances, there is a need for both co-ordination and individual initiative. There is frequently confusion and duplication. The problems can only be overcome by inspired leadership at all levels of the relief operation. In the field, commitment and innovation are essential counterparts to disciplined teamwork at the national level. Too often there is either co-ordination or initiative, but rarely both. Either co-ordination works and decision-making gets over-centralized, or more often it does not. In which case acts of ingenuity at the field level, to get by and make do, take place. But an essentially chaotic and inefficient use of resources occurs.

Relief work requires planning of a high quality. Barring dramatic responses such as the airlift at the start of the Ethiopian operation (a Hercules can only carry twenty-one tonnes of grain – Ethiopia needs 1.5 million tonnes of food aid) bulk food aid can take up to four months or more to arrive at its destination from the moment of request. Therefore, there must be forward planning of needs. In Africa's circumstances of poor infrastructure, other elements must be covered in any plan. Sufficient warehousing must be available; trucks must be on hand – large trucks to move the food to regional warehouses and then smaller, perhaps four-wheel drive ones, to move the food across country to the villages and relief camps. Donors must stage their deliveries so that food does not arrive all at once. Ethiopia's three ports have been working flat out to handle 3,500 tonnes a day, their maximum capacity. In order that ships are not kept waiting for weeks to unload, or alternatively that the ports are not left idle, schedules involving shipments from many different places have to be set up. Even though the biggest individual donors include a country, the United States, and a regional institution, the European Economic Community (EEC), the role of the UN food agency, the World Food Programme (WFP) in co-ordinating these shipments is vital.

Equally, in countries where there are not enough medical staff, it can hardly be left to each agency to decide for itself where it is going to work. There must be careful planning and monitoring of the deployment of all resources, both staff and supplies. In this case a co-ordinating committee of the voluntary agencies, which provide the medical staff, working in conjunction with the national health ministry, may be the best forum for these decisions. Nevertheless, the imperative is the same. In the donor countries, agencies thrive on the inference that they are going off to save the victims of a disaster single-handedly. Yet in the affected country, their effectiveness will depend on their willingness to pool their resources in a disciplined international effort.

When people are forced to move in large numbers from their normal homes, their usual coping mechanisms are gone. They cannot be relied on to know for themselves the level of the river they may have become dependent on for their water. Perhaps it will drop suddenly during the dry season. Nor, if they are unused to being part of a large concentration of people, will they necessarily know the health dangers of using the same water source for bathing and drinking. Relief management requires the highest skills at all levels; and very different skills to those of the development worker. The relief worker cannot place the same faith in the local knowledge of those being helped.

There are rarely sufficient experienced staff available in a famine-affected country; relief agencies bring their own staff with them. It is important, however, that their role is limited in duration and that their lines to a national relief command structure are understood. Occasionally, governments attempt to go it alone and demand aid be handed over to them for distribution. This can hardly be acceptable to agencies because they are accountable to their own publics and because their expertise and experience come to the fore in times of crisis.

In this sense, relief is clearly different from development. Famine is a failure of the development process and requires special measures. African governments need not spurn such external manpower assistance by strenuously insisting on their right to manage their own affairs. That right is not in question. But a famine means their management capacity requires, at least temporarily, to be strengthened. This in no way negates the point; indeed, it confirms that longer term development can only proceed by building up indigenous management capabilities.

Providing a disciplined frame for foreign intervention during a disaster is not easy. It must respect the authority of the national government without skirting round the blunt fact that the international community is there because the national government could not cope. It must also marry disparate, often competing, foreign agencies of varying competence and methods of approach. Often, the agencies are as prickly about their 'sovereignty' as any government. In many cases the quality of their staff leaves a lot to be desired.

The United Nations is expected to provide the leadership, or co-ordination role. This is because as an intergovernmental organization with universal membership, it is the most convenient intermediary between the foreign aid community and national governments.

The agencies within the UN system have a wide variety

of experience and resources to offer. These include the Food and Agriculture Organization (FAO), the World Health Organization (WHO), the UN Children's Fund (UNICEF), the Office of the United Nations Disaster Relief Co-ordinator (UNDRO), and the United High Commissioner for Refugees (UNHCR) and programmes such as the World Food Programme (WFP) and the UN Development Programme (UNDP). However, there is a serious problem of co-ordination between them.

Ironically, at a time when the UN system as a whole is losing authority because of the general failure of governments to strengthen multilateral co-operation, the humanitarian operations have gained respect, not so much because of their competence, but because bilateral donors and other agencies are forced to recognize that the UN has a unique diplomatic ability to intervene with governments of disaster-affected countries.

A weakness of the UN system, however, is that it has no logistic corps of its own. It has its expert agencies on refugees, food, clean water, or children, but not on trucking, often the key dimension in relief operations and certainly so in the case of Africa today.

WFP, as the UN food-moving agency, is accumulating transport experience. But it is not responsible for moving blankets, water or medicines. Somewhere within the system the UN needs to develop a more integrated transport capacity.

Often, the UN is not able to get in early enough. The best relief operations are those which respond to an early warning system and head off famine. The UN is necessarily reactive because of its inter-governmental character. It is reluctant to go in until it is asked. As long as the member states of the UN seek to limit the scope of global inter-governmental co-operation and insist on the pre-eminence of state prerogatives, the full potential of the UN system cannot be brought into play. Reasoning based on state prerogatives is sometimes used also to stop interventions where a government may clearly be failing to deal with a disaster.

Because the UN meets the cost of its disaster work from voluntary contributions from governments, its initial response is also often limited. Most agencies have emergency funds which they can draw on, but these are relatively small. So UN agencies start late and slow.

African governments did, from 1982 and 1983, become increasingly alarmed by the escalating food crisis and can justifiably argue that their warnings were only partially heeded by the international donor community. They were not the ones who were slow to sound the alarm.

Yet in a number of countries where the crisis was first felt there was only limited access to the areas where the hunger was worst, because the government's authority was being challenged by armed opponents. The deterioration in food production is not going to be turned round overnight. Therefore the frequency of food crises will not lessen, and unless the UN is able to insist on full access to hungry areas, whatever the prevailing situation, international action to avert famine is likely to be too late.

The UN could and should be given an anticipatory role. On humanitarian matters it can expect greater sympathy from governments than for instance in the complex field of human rights. Yet even the latter has begun to show results in its commitment to the individual. In the area of humanitarian relief, more could be done to ensure that the UN is enabled to enter hungry areas where control is disputed.

Up to 3000 famine victims a day were leaving Northern Ethiopia in the first months of 1985. The UN did its best to help them when they arrived in Sudan. But the objections of the Ethiopians prevented the UN taking assistance in to the victims in their home areas before they were forced to start the trek out to dependence on foreign food aid in camps far from home. This was because the Ethiopian government has been locked in a bitter struggle with Eritrean rebels for twenty-three years and with the Tigreans for ten years. The conflict has not let up because of the famine. The UN has been unable to insist on a ceasefire to allow an effective relief operation in the famine-hit areas.

In the African famine, the UN has been unable to act as a truly global agency. Its effectiveness would be enhanced if donors would drop their political differences and work together for a humanitarian cause. In Ethiopia, there is practical co-operation in a joint plane and helicopter supply drop to inaccessible mountain areas, organized by the UN and involving donors from East and West. It is an example to emulate.

African countries, which have escaped the drought, obviously do not have much to spare for their less lucky neighbours. Their food position is for the most part only marginally better. And a country like Sudan has been a remarkably generous host to new famine victims from Ethiopia and Chad at the same time that it has a food crisis of its own. The north African countries have given generously. Ghana and others have also contributed to famine relief. However, the non-famine affected countries in Africa have not as a whole been engaged as constructively as they could have been in dealing with the crisis.

The Organization of African Unity (OAU) at its summit in Addis Ababa in 1984 was preoccupied with the famine. Yet the OAU has been unable to play as effective a role as it might have. It does not have the resources, although it has launched its own appeal, for practical assistance. It could provide firmer political backing to international relief efforts. Without real African solidarity to buttress its interventions, the UN is weakened in dealing with individual African governments. Now would be the moment for African leaders as a group to have urged the UN to put people before governments in the race to save lives and to take the food to wherever it was needed.

Given these limits on its authority, any operational weaknesses of the UN are not unsurprising. The Office for Emergency Operations in Africa, established in New York to co-ordinate UN-wide efforts as well as those of the voluntary agencies and other donors, was hurriedly put together in December 1984 when earlier co-ordination efforts were clearly unsatisfactory.

This response was simply ad-hoc. It may work well – such initiatives sometimes have in the past. But it should not be necessary. Where disasters are complex and involve a number of different UN agencies there should be a well-tried process, rather than a last-minute patch-up job, for ensuring a co-ordinated response.

This ad-hocracy impinges directly on the incapacity of the UN to move sooner. The Secretary-General appointed a special representative for the African situation a year earlier but it was only in December 1984, two months after BBC television told the rest of the world what the UN had known full well for eighteen months at least, that this emergency operations office was established. Its full-scale international conference on the African famine came in March 1985. By this time the rains had returned to many countries and the others were well into the present famine year.

This is clearly less than Africa or the international community deserves in this moment of crisis. As a bridge between African needs and the desires of those outside who seek to help, the present machinery of international relief needs to be considerably strengthened.

We have argued that relief operations are unavoidable in the foreseeable future. Famine prediction and prevention do not yet offer a convincing alternative and the short-term prospects for food production and further environmental deterioration suggest further food-supply breakdowns. So, although it has less lasting benefit than development assistance, relief is here to stay.

It does, however, offer possibilities. Famines have a profound effect on societies, causing lasting change. Relief can channel some of this change towards progressive improvements. However, relief operations remain inadequately run. The stage at which disasters could be contained is virtually overlooked in favour of delayed but large-scale relief operations.

An opportunity for common action is being overlooked in all this. The criticisms we offer are widely shared both inside African governments and in the UN. If the moment is seized, this famine can provide an opportunity for fresh appraisal and reform. If that can be rescued from the present disaster, there is hope for the future. In the next chapter we show how it is the neglect and the impoverishment of the countryside that has led to famine.

4 Roots of famine

Famine seems to be the last, the most dreadful resource of nature. The power of population is so superior to the power of the earth to provide subsistence . . . that premature death must in some shape or another visit the human race.

Thomas Malthus, 1798

Life has always been precarious in Africa. Its sub-Saharan region contains twenty-nine of the world's thirty-six poorest countries. Since 1982 a succession of poor harvests, first in southern Africa and then a year later in other parts of sub-Saharan Africa as well, has sent a number of countries plunging below a habitual level of widespread hunger into one of mass starvation.

Many are looking to the meteorologists for indications as to when the famine will lift: will it rain throughout the region as it now has in southern Africa? But rain by itself is not enough. By early 1985, twenty African countries were seeking emergency food aid. Over centuries, societies learnt to live within the constraints of their environment. Rain may have always been erratic in Africa and topsoil thin, and in a country like Ethiopia famine is frequent. But famine on anything like the present scale probably never occurred.

Poor people are always worse affected by disasters, be it flood, drought, earthquake, volcano, hurricane, gas leak or whatever. It is their vulnerability which exposes them to the full force of a disaster. The disaster itself may strike all in its path, but those more likely to be huddled unprotected in its way are the poor, because they cannot afford to be anywhere else. People with means live in well-built, well-located houses and can afford to buy food even if the crops fail.

Famine, a short-term phenomenon, is inescapably linked to persistent long-term poverty. Rich people don't starve. The idea of famines wiping out whole societies, as though the consequences of bad weather were meted out in equal measure to all, is far-fetched and can usually be traced to sensationalist history writing rather than a real record of what happened. Recent exponents of the linkage between poverty and famines have dispelled some of the myths surrounding this historical view of famine as nature's leveller, striking out indiscriminately at classes and societies that meteorological chance causes it to alight on.

At the height of the present crisis, Africa is still growing the majority of the food it consumes. Even in famines there is always some food. Who has ever seen a starving military officer or merchant, let alone aid worker? It is a question of who has access to that food.

Famines do not occur only when there is less food available. In Bangladesh in 1974, when a large number of famine deaths occurred, there was in fact more food than there had been a year earlier. However, the experience of shortages and the prospects of further ones persuaded those with food to hoard it until the prices went up. Such an argument might seem academic when there is not enough food to go round, as is the case in Africa at present, but the analysis is vital because its implication is that as agricultural production revives, poor people will not necessarily stop starving.

They may be livestock owners who had to give away their cattle at knockdown prices during the drought to buy grain for their own consumption; or farmers whose crop failed and who therefore do not now have the income to buy food or seed even when it is available again; or urban workers who have lost their jobs in a recession. All these groups can be found amongst famine victims.

It is clear that some governments in Africa have been unable to prevent food speculation. Some of the richest families in the Indian state of Bengal made their fortunes during the famine in 1943. Similar fortunes are currently being made in Africa and there is no doubt that the lasting impact on the African political economy of each cycle of famine is an increase in the gap between the rich and the poor. After the Sahel famine in the 1970s, there was a marked shift of livestock ownership from the small herdsmen to absentee merchants.

So, although this book is about Africa and the famine there, the basic link of disaster and poverty has a much wider application. Rain failures happen everywhere. Even the world's main grain exporter, the United States, is not immune – a drought in its farming lands is a predictable event every twenty years or so. But American farmers don't starve, their politicians and bank managers see to that. In fact in the early months of 1985, additional famine relief for Africa was held up in the United States Congress, because politicians hoped to graft on to it credit help for America's farmers, who were hard-pressed because they have been growing too much rather than too little food.

In Africa population growth is steadily outstripping increases in food production. While population is increasing at about 3.1 per cent a year, food production was, during the five years until the drought, increasing at about 1.6 per cent a year. Malnutrition, which was the regular

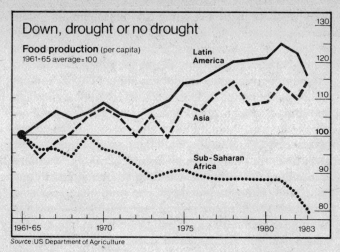

Down, drought or no drought

Food production (per capita)
1961-65 average=100

Latin America

Asia

Sub-Saharan Africa

130
120
110
100
90
80

1961-65   1970   1975   1980   1983

Source: US Department of Agriculture

Figure I

condition of about eighty million people at the onset of the last major African famine between 1972–74, is now the routine fate of over 100 million. In those countries where the food shortages are now worst, food production per head of population has been falling over the last fourteen years at an average of 2 per cent a year. Figure I illustrates this divergence between the rates of growth in food production and population.

Drought, in terms of the amount of locally grown food available per person, just brought forward a moment which would have been reached anyway in 1988. The trend over the last two decades has been irresistibly downwards. The food deficit, that is the gap between what is grown and what is needed for consumption, is steadily growing, drought or no drought.

The countries where the food shortages have been worst should cause no surprise. They are those countries which had already been marked out in land-use surveys as unable to support their existing population employing their present level of agriculture. Ethiopia's poverty makes it peculiarly prone to disaster. Taking the new census figures, it seems the average income is only about $110 per annum, the lowest in Africa. Life expectancy is forty-seven years. The literacy rate is only about 45 per cent and a survey some years ago showed that only 6 per cent of the people have access to safe water. Until the famine, Ethiopia was, apart from considerable amounts of food aid, getting very little external development assistance. According to one calculation, Ethiopia was in 1982 receiving only $6 per head in official development assistance compared to about $18 for sub-Saharan Africa as a whole.

Ethiopian food shortages are so chronic that the government has appealed for help every year for the last eleven years. Its history is littered with records of famine, not least because, until the 1974 revolution, its élite city life rested on one of the most exploitative systems of land tenure in Africa.

Its structure always prevented peasants achieving their own food security as many of their counterparts elsewhere in the continent were able to do. Between 1540 and 1800, twenty-three major famines were recorded; the great famine of 1888–92 was in its scale a forebear of what has happened in 1984–5.

But historical comparisons should not hide the truth that modern changes in Africa have sharply increased the degree of vulnerability to famine. On average, more than six times as many people around the world died each year from disasters in the 1970s compared to the 1960s. These figures, compiled in a Swedish Red Cross study, are not statistically very satisfactory but, however incomplete, they show a trend which has continued into the 1980s.

There are proportionately many times more deaths from disasters in low income countries as in middle and high income ones. Africa is reaping the consequences not just of weather, but of poverty.

The amount of poverty in Africa is increasing. The World Bank, using as its standard an annual income of less than $135 (at 1980 values), projected that in Africa the number of people living in poverty is likely to increase by 70 per cent by the end of the century. This compares with its overall sample of forty developing countries where there was some hope that the number of poor would fall by a third. In China, economic reform, support for small-scale farming, aggressive wealth-redistribution policies, and forceful family planning, mean that this vast country is likely to have achieved a decline of 80–90 per cent in the number of its poor by the year 2000.

In a report on the 1973–74 famine, the present Ethiopian government concluded that, 'the primary source of the famine was not a drought of unprecedented severity but a combination of long-continued bad land use and steadily increased human and stock populations over decades, rendering a greater number of people and their animals vulnerable when drought struck.' Not enough has changed since then.

The African agricultural record as a whole compares unfavourably with that of others. China, for example, was by 1980–82 producing 124 per cent more food per head than it was eleven years earlier, whereas Ethiopia was producing less than 80 per cent, Mali 83 per cent, Tanzania 88 per cent, Somalia 60 per cent and Zimbabwe 87 per cent. There are exceptions. For example Burundi, Rwanda and Malawi, all of which are small countries with higher population concentrations, have, unlike many of their vast underpopulated neighbours, managed to keep food production just about abreast of population growth. Yet Africa has the land to feed a much larger population than it presently has.

Historically, rural impoverishment has been one spur to the creation of a new industrial proletariat. But in African cities, there are not enough jobs. There are alarming indications that Africa's economic transition may be longer, less certain and, in its present form, abortive. In such circumstances, the disaster syndrome, in the form of drought and poverty leading to uncontainable famine, will recur frequently.

In 1980, less than 20 per cent of the population in the low-income group of African countries was urban. Yet that town population is expected to increase proportionately more rapidly than elsewhere in the world in the next fifteen years – at a rate of 6 per cent a year. In the richer sub-Saharan African countries already a much higher proportion of the population is made up of town-dwellers. It is a potential demographic snare for the region. Certainly, people will not be escaping disaster by moving from the famine-prone countryside to the towns. They will be taking their vulnerability with them. Without a secure farming base and with urban activities, in many cases, getting off to a spluttering start, the amount of deprivation in both town and countryside could increase markedly. The World Bank now believes that the sub-Saharan population of 385 million in 1980 will have at least doubled by 2005. Given the economic prospects of these countries this trend will add to the pool of the poor and disaster-prone unless there is radical change in these countries' plans for economic growth. The differences between economic strength and population growth are starkly illustrated in maps III and IV.

Africa must expect – even if it takes major steps now to

push family planning and other steps to manage the demographic explosion – that its population growth will outstrip the capacity of its economies to create jobs or of its governments to care for the extra population well into the next century. The present growth rate in sub-Saharan Africa is 3.1 per cent (4 per cent in places).

Of Ethiopia's current population of 42 million, 7.9 million cannot feed themselves this year, according to the UN, and depend on international generosity. Population specialists claim the country's population could increase as much as seven times before it stabilizes. At which point the population of this soil-eroded country would be more than that of the United States today. How many will then be starving? The uncomfortable fact is that countries with stable populations, the industrialized societies, are increasingly having to help feed many of those with fast-growing populations, particularly in Africa.

Nigeria's working-age population will have doubled by the end of the century. Government resources will have difficulty keeping pace. In Malawi, assuming teachers' salaries and other costs do not increase in real terms, the budget for primary education will still have to double every fifteen years. African education is already sparse and under-financed. In 1978 it took 16 per cent of national budgets and only reached two-thirds of children of primary school age.

An initiative to bring population growth into better balance with economic opportunity must begin from an understanding of social pressures for population growth in Africa. Children still represent extra hands for the fields, security for old age, a symbol of potency and, in some societies, a link for the spirit of parents, when they die, with life. Contraceptive methods are not widely accepted.

In the eighteenth century, 20 per cent of the world's

Population growth

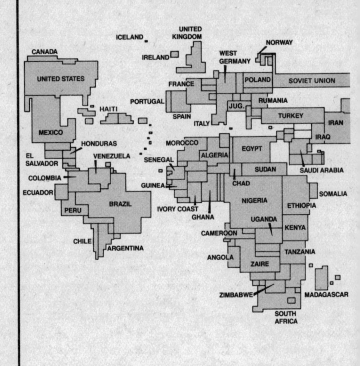

Map III

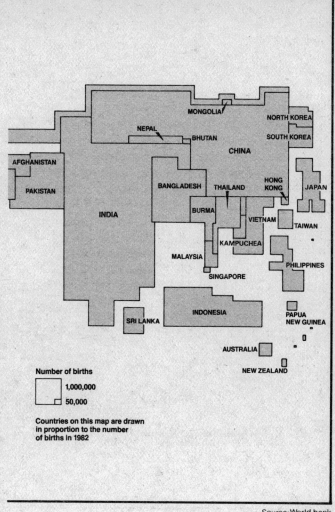

Number of births

☐ 1,000,000

▫ 50,000

Countries on this map are drawn
in proportion to the number
of births in 1982

Source: World bank

ECONOMIC STRENGTH

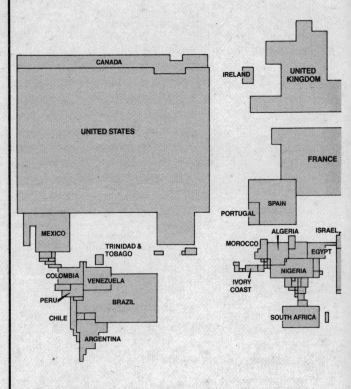

Those countries for which data not available
(or population less than 1m) not shown

Also not every country name shown

Map IV

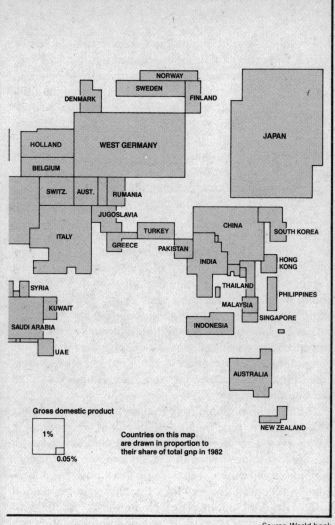

Gross domestic product

1%

0.05%

Countries on this map
are drawn in proportion to
their share of total gnp in 1982

Source: World bank

population lived in Africa. Even with the present high rates of growth it is likely to be less than 13 per cent in the year 2000.

Another factor is the problem of infertility in central Africa. Whereas in developing countries as a whole only 2–3 per cent of women past childbearing age are childless, surveys in the 1950s and 1960s in eighteen African countries showed that 12 per cent of older women had had no children. The highest such rates were in the Central African Republic, Cameroon, Zaire, Congo and Gabon. In parts of Zaire the rate was as high as 65 per cent. A major reason is the prevalence of untreated sexually transmitted diseases.

So for many reasons, pressing the case for family planning is not easy – the social climate favours a baby boom. Such pressures operate in a context where the real constraints on economic growth often appear to be the emptiness of the land rather than its over-population. To many, it appears that there is plenty of under-used land. It just happens to be where people are not. Not that the availability of spare land in itself is an answer to a population explosion. Also, markets are often too far away and customers too scarce to provide much incentive to the rural entrepreneur. And the population is too scattered for innovation or co-operation to catch on. In fact, Africans are alternatively crowded on to overused lands and in some areas spread too thin.

The population issue is crucial to this report, not just because it is a time-bomb that threatens all progress in Africa, but also because it is one that is amenable to outside assistance. African leaders are, as a statement they made at Arusha, Tanzania, in 1984 indicated, beginning to recognize the need for establishing a population policy. It does not need much power of foresight to recognize that the cycle of falling incomes and rising absolute poverty will not be broken unless the rate of population growth is checked.

Outside assistance can help determined African leadership by providing funds for census-taking (the result of which can raise the problem on the national agenda), for family planning clinics and for the other inputs which will bring viable strategies to bear at the community level. Each society will find its own most acceptable ways of restraining family size, perhaps marrying later, or increasing the intervals between children, or where there is polygamy, having fewer wives. But modern methods of contraception available free, or at subsidised prices, and modern mother and child health care clinics to increase the survival chances of children and therefore reduce the incentives for having extra ones, will be vital. The experience in Latin America and Asia shows outsiders cannot impose solutions. To attempt to influence family relations is counterproductive. But community leaders can set the tone and establish the goals, and foreign aid can support and encourage these initiatives where local resources are scarce. Wherever there is a sign of more favourable official or community attitudes to family planning in Africa, aid agencies would do well to nurture and back them. It is an essential gamble on Africa's future.

So the prospects for Africa's poor of avoiding future famines must be weighed against a background of inadequate food production, increasing population, and a movement of people to the towns. It is the increasing incidence of poverty in Africa which separates it from other parts of the developing world and raises the real prospect of further famines. The world has enough to eat. The difficulty is that nations and individuals often lack the means to purchase it. The World Bank's World Development Report for 1984 supports this view: '. . . the main issue is not the worldwide availability of food, but the capacity of nations, groups within nations, and individuals to obtain enough food for a healthy diet'.

Africa, and Africans, are at the back of the line. In the next chapter we look at how the environment, on which African rural life depends, is in crisis. Its deterioration deepens the level of poverty.

5 Deterioration

Trees are the earth's endless effort to speak to the listening heavens.

Rabindranath Tagore, 1928

To those who do not know Africa, the two images of its terrain which spring to mind are steaming tropical forests and deserts. It is not that simple. Africa has less than 15 per cent of the world's tropical forest cover, and much of that is in just one African country, Zaire. The Sahara desert, the principle desert of the continent, is a thick belt stretching out across Africa from the north-west. And in south-western Africa, there is the Kalahari. There are fertile farming lands in many parts of Africa, however. The desert is not all-embracing. Between the two deserts is the Intertropical Convergence Zone (ITCZ), the band of wet weather which circles the world at the point where the trade winds blowing from the northern and southern hemispheres meet. During the year, this band moves first north and then south, with the passage of the earth around the sun, bringing rain as it moves.

The countries at the limits of its trajectory get a single rainy season, while those it passes over twice have two. Its two boundaries are the Sahara in the north and the Kalahari in the south. Those countries on the fringe of the deserts are very dry indeed, and it is these which have taken the full brunt of the drought. Even in years of average rainfall, the shortage of water limits their agricultural possibilities.

Broadly speaking, for Africa as a whole, almost half is considered by FAO to be too dry for crop cultivation. But of the land that is suitable, only a small part is being used.

For the equatorial countries in between the two dry belts at either end of the zone, water supply is more plentiful but still unreliable. The rain is spread unevenly throughout the year. At times there are storms of furious intensity. Huge, fast raindrops can smash the soil surface, blocking the 'pores' through which water could be absorbed. Much of the precious water simply runs off farmers' lands, often taking topsoil with it. In the tropical heat, the water which remains quickly evaporates, so even countries with a higher average annual rainfall than Britain can look drought-stricken for part of the year. So it is not always just a matter of too little water.

However, in much of Africa towards the two edges of the zone, there is not only too little rainfall, it is also irregular. Since a high proportion of Africa's rain comes from local evaporation (that means it is recycled from previous rainfall), a pattern of poor rainfall can become persistent.

The warmer the climate the quicker the degradation of organic matter. This is because it cannot accumulate in the soil in a thick layer as it can in colder climates. Taken together with the rainfall problems, Africa's soil needs all the protection of careful human management it can get. An environmental strategy for Africa has to have two main parts, protecting soils and protecting trees. They are inter-related.

The most luxuriant forests of the world in fact grow on the poorest soils. If the forest cover is torn away, soils are depleted of their humus and the combination of heavy rainfall and sunshine transform the upper layer into a thick and hard crust of 'laterite' which is impossible to plough for cultivation. Management of nature is therefore much more difficult than in temperate zones where deforestation does not sterilize the land in this way.

In seeking to stop deforestation a basic psychological barrier has to be crossed. For many local people, forests are still synonymous with backwardness and clearing them for cultivation appears to be an elementary first step to improving one's lot. Forests are a source of isolation, inconvenience and often disease. The modern peasant cultivator is often ill at ease in a forest, with little idea of how to live in harmony with it. Too often the value of the forest is not recognized by those to whom it affords protection and fuel until it is too late. For instance, in Europe and North America, the destruction of the forests had reached the penultimate stage before any real environmental consciousness developed.

The daily demands of wood for the farm, or of a space for a new field, might seem to be of more importance to the family living next to woodland than long-term environmental concerns. Conservation has to be married to realistic exploitation of forests, hence the need for sensible forest management. Trees must quite simply be cut at a rate which does not run way ahead of the speed at which new forest cover can replace them. Trees can be cut but the crisis of deforestation in Africa comes about because exploitation has been reckless, and unplanned.

With the exception of the massive moist tropical forests in Zaire, and a handful of smaller ones elsewhere, forest conservation in Africa is principally to do with protecting open woodland as a barrier against the deterioration of the soil.

The overwhelming thrust of aid and private finance in forestry has been towards the exploitation rather than the preservation of forests. It has not been a happy role. Wood has been considered a resource that could earn some African countries, particularly those in West Africa, vital foreign exchange. The rate at which tree cover has been lost in this region is astonishing. Large areas which were covered by trees 200 years ago are now practically bare.

However, commercial exploitation has not been the main source of deforestation in Africa. Even in the Ivory Coast, the continent's main timber exporter, for every cubic metre of wood cut down by industry, 4.5 cubic metres has been destroyed by those clearing land for farming. Of the twelve million hectares of dense forest cover that existed, only two million remain.

The small cultivators have been their own worst enemy in terms of the abuse of forest. More than 90 per cent of the wood used in Africa is for cooking and other energy needs. In many African countries the style of rural life is being profoundly changed by the firewood crisis. An increasing number of a family's working hours are taken up going ever further afield in search of firewood. For centuries people lived in balance with their energy source, cutting wood at a rate at which it could be renewed. Reforestation must take account of the trees local people want for their combined needs of fuel, agroforestry, diet, soil protection, and so on. Also trees must be chosen which will grow quickly enough to meet the needs of an expanding population. But local people should be listened to. Already there are tree planta-tions, fostered by external assistance, where the wrong trees have been planted and the plantations left untended because nobody wants them.

There is obviously also a big role for more fuel-efficient stoves. Many are now available. The ones that have 'taken best' are those that were designed in full consultation with the end-user, the rural African. Cultural concerns, like an open flame for the family to gather round in the evening, and a stove which can provide the right intensity of heat for cooking the dishes of the particular local diet must be taken account of.

However, even if there are individual tree projects, innovative stoves and such like, protecting the forests is not a serious national policy in many of the countries at risk. In some this is because they have other preoccupations, in others, like Sudan, it is because despite a real determination to do something, the government does not have the funds.

The other aspect, intimately linked to success in protecting trees, is saving soils. At the margin of the deserts, economic and social changes have disrupted the fragile balance between livestock and the vegetation cover, leading to the spread of deserts. The top soil of Africa is being rapidly lost. The Sahara, particularly, is spreading with alarming rapidity. The United Nations estimates that the Sahara's front line is advancing at 1.5 million hectares (3.7 million acres) a year.

For those on the front, for example in Western Sudan, this means a desert advance of some six kilometres a year. El Fasher, a regional capital, used to be surrounded by cultivated fields, now the visitor flying crosses desert on all sides. The image is of a city under siege by the sand.

But, as we have pointed out, Africa is not all desert or lush jungle. As typical are the scrub, woodlands and barely green savannah lands of so much of the continent. This is not the rich, well-irrigated farmland that covers great expanses of Latin America and Asia. African soils are for the most part fragile and lower in nutrients, something which has been overlooked by those who have transplanted European methods of agriculture. Patches of desertification break out across the fragile lands of sub-Saharan

Africa, wherever land is over-used, and is not limited to the ever-broadening rim of the desert itself. The great forward march of the Sahara itself has a mesmerising effect, but focusing on that, as many donors have, risks overlooking the outbreaks of desertification across the continent. Even the rich farming lands of Kenya are not immune. Too intensive European farming methods and overpopulated areas of traditional African cultivation have taken a toll there too.

There are meteorologists who argue that the level of rainfall in the Sahel states has been diminishing over the last fifteen years or so, and it seems that the traditionally wettest month, August, has become dryer in recent years. The impression of those in Sudan is that the crop-growing season in the dryer areas is being constricted by an increasingly short rainy season. The difficulty with such claims is that there seem to be disagreements about the quality of evidence. In fact, there have been some rather good sets of rainfall data collected but whether or not they are comprehensive and comparable enough to reach general conclusions is in doubt. Obviously, there has been a lot less rain than usual in the last few years but whether that marks the low point of a normal cycle, or is indeed a break with all past weather patterns is still open to doubt.

What is certain is that environmental deterioration, once set in motion, can become self-reinforcing although the reasons for this are only partly understood. The loss of vegetation cover adversely affects the amount of rainfall, and as the former depends on rain its own decline is also then speeded up. The natural environment is never a neutral and passive force in the life people make for themselves. People and nature interact. That interaction has become dangerously unhinged in contemporary Africa.

Today, methods of agriculture often reinforce the consequences of weather failure rather than providing the means of coping with it. This is dealt with at greater length in the next chapter.

There has been little effective action to counter the spread of the desert. The only attempt to do something coherent was the plan that came out of the United Nations Conference on Desertification in 1977. It represented the combined efforts of the representatives of 95 countries, 50 UN bodies and 65 non-governmental organizations.

Very much a child of its time, it reflected the hope that donors could invest large quantities of capital aid. It presumed that African governments could mobilize resources to reverse the environmental deterioration. The plan reflected the shopping list mentality of aid at that time. There was a long list of expensive projects of variable quality. Nevertheless, the plan of action was a comprehensive package, which, had it been implemented, would by now be allowing some initiative to be regained over the rapidly deteriorating environment. Where there are governments with the means and the will such as China, the Soviet Union and the United States, impressive gains have been made in containing desertification.

Nobody can quarrel with either the spirit of the plan or the immediate priorities that were set: sound land use; improved livestock raising; better farming methods; rehabilitation of irrigation schemes and environmental conservation measures. In addition, there was a series of proposed investigations to improve understanding of the causes of desertification and to find remedies. But the irony is that a lot can be done to hold the desert at bay by applying existing knowledge. It is not the know-how that is lagging behind so much as the practical application.

In Asia, Latin America and Africa, voluntary agencies

and community groups are embarking on small-scale tree-planting schemes, water conservation projects and much else – the fundamentals of protecting the land. Certainly recent successes in land reclamation in China, the Soviet Union and the United States have involved major government action. But the whole experience of combating desertification shows that, even if there is still debate over its causes, a mobilization of local farmers to meet the desert head-on with trees, water-management and traditional cropping techniques is effective. A preoccupation with large government schemes has left this 'grassroots' approach ignored for too long.

In May 1984, the governing council of the UN Environment Programme (UNEP) assessed what had been achieved since the plan of action was adopted in 1977. UNEP had to report that virtually none of the recommendations had been carried out. A hundred countries round the world have a desert problem. In Africa, only Sudan, and elsewhere only Afghanistan, have prepared national desertification plans along the lines agreed in 1977. UNEP reported: 'This inadequate organizational response is reflected in generally poor progress in national assessments of desertification, despite international and regional assistance, and in a general failure to formulate effective national plans to combat desertification.'

Of the six major transnational projects which were recommended, no action has ever been taken on four. Only two, both in fact in Africa, are said by UNEP to have been started in any form at all.

Of those planned, only two of the regional research and development centres have been set up. These are the Sahel Institute in Mali and a regional agro-meteorology and hydrology centre in Niger. Knowledge of the extent of desertification, and of the area at greatest risk, has hardly improved at all since 1977.

Globally, the problem has actually less been a matter of absolute resources devoted to fighting desertification and more how the money has been spent. One researcher believes that $10 billion was spent through the major agencies between 1978 and 1983. Certainly this was less than what was apparently required but the trouble was that a good deal of this considerable investment did not go into projects with the highest priority: those that would have stopped the desert at the local level. Instead the money was used to improve national and regional infrastructure and various back-up services and only a small part of the funds went into improving the frontline day-to-day interaction of small farmer and desert.

Even if the money for desertification control and its impact have been disappointing, the eight countries of the Sahel have enjoyed an aid boom. Their combined population of thirty million is not huge but until Ethiopia burst on the international conscience, their precarious life on dry land was some sort of symbol to outsiders of Africa's problems. The Sahel provides an interesting, although extreme, case study of why aid has not stopped the desert in Africa. More has been spent, probably less efficiently, than anywhere else in sub-Saharan Africa. The Organization for Economic Co-operation and Development (OECD) and multilateral donors set up the Club du Sahel in Paris for directing aid to the Sahel countries. The desert is a good fund-raiser. It is just that the money often follows wrong priorities.

Some $14 billion will have been committed to eight Sahel states in the decade ending 1984. That is $44 per head per year, compared to $18 for sub-Saharan Africa as a whole. Aid now amounts to 17 per cent of the Sahelian group's gross domestic product (GDP), and accounts for over 80 per cent of its external resources. Up-to-date figures are not available, but by 1980 at least $2 billion of aid was in the form of long-term loans, increasing Sahelian indebtedness (although on concessional terms) by some 60 per cent.

Niger was the only Sahel country to have avoided a food crisis during 1984. It has a good record of seeking to pursue food self-sufficiency strategies. But its luck, and good management, did not hold out into 1985 when its food shortages and the subsequent human migration made it one of the worst crisis points on the continent.

In the Sahel states, as much as amongst their neighbours, the desert presses on despite the foreign aid. It is now estimated that more than 90 per cent of pasture and 85 per cent of crop lands in the nineteen sub-Saharan countries closest to the Sahara are affected by desertification.

So what have aid-givers sought to do about it? In the sub-Saharan savannah where rainfall is always scarce, irrigation might seem the obvious way of increasing agricultural production. Irrigation schemes have absorbed 15 per cent of all aid spent. By 1980, more than 2.5 million hectares in the Sahel were under irrigation. The Senegal river basin scheme, which is intended to provide some 350,000 hectares of irrigated land, is expected to cost more than $1 billion. Sceptics point to a failure rate in such projects of at least 25 per cent, because the irrigated soil becomes saline, drainage is not properly maintained and there are equipment problems. There are also doubts about whether there will be enough water for such ambitious schemes. Further evidence of a real climatic shift is that water levels in rivers such as the Senegal, Niger, and Chari appear, according to some experts, to have been steadily dropping in recent years. Irrigated agriculture can encourage patterns of settlement that are not realistic. The nomads of the Sahel may thus be encouraged to move into fixed settlements and over-intensive use of land may then follow.

Where irrigated schemes do work, crop production is too often turned over to rice for the towns and cash crops for export before local food production is secure. Rain-fed, as against irrigated, agriculture has received only 4.5 per cent of Sahelian aid although it accounts for 95 per cent of cereal production.

Simplistic, quick solutions, favoured by donors and governments anxious to throw money at the desert, do not have a happy record. It took several years before the popular well drilling programmes of the mid-1970s were found, in many cases, to contribute to desertification by encouraging high concentrations of people and animals at the water points.

In the Sahel, only 24 per cent of aid has gone towards agriculture and forestry – but less than half of that was spent on actual rural agricultural and forestry projects. In these countries the vast majority of the populations live in the countryside, 91 per cent in Burkina Faso, 87 per cent in Niger, 83 per cent in Mali and 82 per cent in Chad. One of the more exciting areas of current research is agroforestry – where crops and trees are interplanted so that the crops get the protection of better soil, with its nitrogen retained.

But that is not where the money went. Instead it went to urban based 'support' projects. Some 28 per cent of the agricultural aid that was given was spent on cash crops, mainly peanuts and cotton. The irony is that a number of Sahel states have had increasing success with cash crops as their food production as a whole falls to the drought. The best irrigated land has been taken by these important foreign exchange earners.

Also, less than 5 per cent of aid has been spent on the

livestock sector. This is particularly surprising given the fact that it is the main source of earnings for most of the Sahel countries. Successful livestock management is one of the key ways of coping with the desert. So while desertification is no slouch as a fund-raiser, too much money has gone on what a report for UNEP described as 'road construction, buildings, water supplies, research, training courses and meetings'. UNEP's own assessment is: 'Four-fifths of investment in projects related to desertification falls into the category of preparatory or supportive actions, with only one-fifth in the category of corrective field action. Even within that category, emphasis has been placed on measures to increase production rather than on arresting desertification processes.'

UNEP's executive director is prepared to go as far as many of the critics: 'Far too much technical and financial assistance has gone to showpiece projects and into measures aimed at appeasing the more politically advantaged urban population.' By comparison, rural populations which tend to lack political clout – especially in the more remote semi-arid regions – are all but ignored. When it comes to allotting funds for rural development, agroforestry and other ecologically sound activities are nearly always at the end of the queue.

What emerges from our analysis of both deforestation and desertification in Africa is that the efforts to avert these processes have mostly fallen at the first fence. UNEP, the agency which although it was never intended to be operational, might have been the mobilizer and co-ordinator of international efforts, has fallen short of what its own leadership would have wanted.

We do not advocate vast new projects to arrest the desert through huge irrigation schemes, or any ostentatious construction schemes in the desert. Instead we plead for a partnership which is modest in its financial dimensions, but far-reaching in its implications. National and international efforts harnessed to the human energies of those who have to live daily with the threat of the encroaching desert, those in the front line, be they herdsman or cultivator. Tools, trees, better seeds, small-scale water conservation, and so on are the weapons for fighting the African desert, not mega-dams. In the next chapter, we discuss a viable agriculture for Africa.

6 Regeneration

Burn down your cities and leave our farms, and your cities will spring up again as if by magic; but destroy our farms and the grasses will grow in the streets of every city in the country.

William Jennings Byran, 1826

The first step is re-financing the rural sector. Protecting the soil and the forest is not in the short-term interest of under-financed small farmers. The small farmer is rightly seen as potentially the most land-careful user of Africa's fragile soils. Yet at the moment the farmer is its greatest abuser.

It is only recently that the potential of mixed cropping and other traditional techniques have been recognized by a research community which was obsessed by European or North American agriculture. Agricultural research needs to be reorientated towards an analysis of the various ecological factors and their relation to the socio-economic character of Africa. Interdisciplinary teams have to work hand in hand with the farmers and herders. This calls for humility in dealing with complexity.

Research during the colonial period was almost entirely devoted to plantation crops – oil palm, coffee, and the like – rather than popular food crops, and to crossing local cattle with temperate breeds to raise meat production. Such experiments produced cattle which need too much care to be suitable for life in the bush. Since 1970, there has been no shortage of funds for research in Africa, but it has still not been sufficiently concentrated on the dryland crops and roots and tubers which poorer people eat. Maize research, for example, has received much greater funding than sorghum or millet which need less water and are therefore more relevant to the drought-prone areas.

International agricultural research centres have been a major contributing factor to the success of Asian agriculture. In Africa, this is less true. Where research is appropriate, the relationship with national research networks is sometimes not close enough for really systematic contact, through these institutions, with the farmers themselves. Often, data is collected in national research centres but seldom analysed. For example, weather statistics of relevance to farmers have been collected in the Sahel since early this century and yet, for lack of funds and co-ordination, they are rarely collated, even though they could greatly improve scientists' certainty about whether or not the area is getting drier.

The usefulness of successful research into African food crops can hardly be overstressed. The most relevant research has always been done by peasant farmers themselves. Anthropological work has shown that local farmers' knowledge of the environment in which they work is highly complex and organized, as are their own experiments with plant and animal breeding. Yet scientists working on the same problems have rarely collaborated in the past with farmers in the field. Research will only be useful if it produces innovations which constitute a reasonable risk for peasant farmers, and which is consistent, rather than at odds, with well-tried traditional techniques.

First the colonial authorities, then local urban elites and aid agencies alike have assumed that peasant farming methods were downright inefficient and that their un-willingness to adopt new technologies was a mark of their ignorance. Such judgements did not look at the innovations from the point of view of the peasant. A high-yielding variety of maize requires fertilizer, pesticides and water to attain its full potential, and if any of these factors is absent, might give a lower yield than the traditional variety. With a limited amount to invest, a poor peasant cannot afford the risk of going into debt to buy the seed and then not being able to pay the debt back when the crop fails for lack of fertilizer or pesticide – or because there is not enough rain. Building on peasant knowledge and needs requires a parti-cipatory approach and a willingness to rough it in the field. Too many scientists still prefer their laboratories.

The technologies on offer from the developed world have often been singularly inappropriate to the needs of small farmers. In the Sahel region, for example, during the 1970s, donors were keen to fund settled cattle ranching projects which failed to raise the incomes of pastoralists or improve the quality of pasture. A recent Dutch study revealed 'that traditional herders produce as much protein per hectare as do ranchers in areas of equal rainfall in the United States and Australia; the Sahelian herders, how-ever, accomplish this with infinitely less mechanical energy inputs, relying for the most part on manpower'. Donors must break the habit of constantly looking down upon local knowledge.

Even while research is being reorientated, and recon-nected with peasant and herder agriculture, there are a number of ways, based on already-known peasant tech-niques, to maintain the fertility of land under shifting agri-culture, and to improve its productivity. These include growing crops between rows of fast-growing trees, which both protect the soil from wind and water erosion, and provide fodder for animals. Small-scale water collecting schemes such as planting crops on ridges which trap water in between, have proved quite successful. Another technique is to sow crops without initially tilling the soil. This reduces the amount of soil erosion. Mixed cropping, where two or more plants are grown simultaneously on one plot, can give higher overall yields than when a single variety is used to cover the whole plot. This practice, used by African farmers for centuries, used to be considered inefficient. But as well as being productive, it is a good form of insurance. If there is a plague of insects, for example, with a partiality for one crop but not another, the farmer's losses are less.

While scientists should look for traditional knowledge there is no reason why this cannot be blended with modern, but appropriate, innovation. After all the land has to bear many more people than it used to. The rural sector must be dynamic but in a way that takes account of ecological constraint and traditional wisdom.

Extension workers, the agricultural workers who work with farmers, must get closer to them in helping to identify and resolve problems. This would diminish their role as the purveyors of official wisdom from the city.

Until now, the small farming sector has been left to its own devices. Governments have been preoccupied with the urban sector and with large-scale and cash-crop farming. Now they need to shift resources to small-scale farming, especially for subsistence food production. But they also cannot easily shift resources away from the urban sector. Botswana, Gambia and Tanzania do plan to increase public investment in agriculture within their existing national plans. Others also intend to redirect resources towards agriculture. In fact, about thirty-five African countries are now preparing, or already have national food strategies. But they all operate under severe financial constraints.

Among the policy changes urged on African governments by donors are more realistic prices for both food and export crops to give the farmer a fair return. The donors, however, do now recognize that these policy changes are not the only key to Africa's agricultural production problems. Higher real prices for what the peasants grow may not always encourage them to produce more. There must be adequate facilities favourable enough to them so that they can both sell their surplus production and become themselves consumers. That means goods must be available in their villages which they would want to spend their extra income on. Transport and storage must be improved. Farmers may have to grow a lot more before they really have spare food to sell, which they do not want to eat, or store, themselves. Higher official prices may actually mean they just sell legally what they were selling on the black market before. Above all, liberalizing food prices without ensuring that the small farmer's position in the grain trade is secure could lead to the power of the big farmer and merchant becoming greater.

The different ways in which peasants might respond to a rise in the prices of the crops they produce reflects that the African peasant as a single category exists only in the minds of non-African observers. Farmers work in infinitely varied surroundings, and relations between farmers are frequently complex. Observers compound the mistake of treating all peasants as the same when they assume that all peasants are men. In some parts of rural Africa, women farmers provide up to 90 per cent of the food. On top of their work on the land, they invariably prepare and cook the food as well. In West Africa, up to 80 per cent of all trade in food is handled by women. Migrant labour, especially in southern Africa, means that today, not only do women do most of the work on farms, they often head rural households during their husbands' prolonged absence. Their work as decision-makers and labourers (and the competing demands on their time made by domestic labour) has been notoriously neglected in past agricultural development efforts. Quite simply, not enough is known.

The rising incomes of some townspeople mean that they invest in agriculture, producing changes in the ownership of rural assets which has been insufficiently taken account of. In Nigeria, subsidised tractors and bank loans to farmers have been easily co-opted by a small class of 'overnight' farmers – urban businessmen, civil servants, district chiefs and army officers. Famine, and consequent rural impoverishment, offers city people further opportunities to buy into the rural sector on the cheap.

The small farmer does not have to fend off only local businessmen: Western multinationals still hold considerable sway. Multinational companies handle much of the processing of cash crops, from the time they leave the African farmer to the moment they reach the consumer overseas. Their influence sways the aid world too. Agribusiness staff pass in and out of the big development agencies such as the World Bank, The United States Agency for International Development (USAID) and the EEC as consultants. With their apparent savvy and local knowledge from many years in Africa, they have kept the candle of large-scale farming alight for too long in the aid world.

And while it would be equally unbalanced to deny any role for large-scale farming, it can safely be said that as a sector, it is well able to look after itself. Large farmers have political influence and access to capital. It is the small-scale sector that needs help.

The challenge now, for donor agencies and governments alike, is to find ways to foster appropriate research and to fund the small, rural institutions – itinerant credit banks, grain storage co-operatives, farmers' seed-testing groups and the like – which will lead to a renaissance of the rural sector. In the past, they have been considered too small to attract donors anxious to keep administrative overheads down by making a few big grants and loans rather than a lot of small ones.

Here we describe an example of sensitive foreign aid to support nomadic pastoralists in Niger. It is far removed from the grandiose schemes which some might still be tempted to recommend to beat back the desert. The nomadic cattle-raisers suffered more than any other people in the Sahel during the 1968 to 1973 drought, but their discomfort did not end when the rains returned. The region was inundated with large-scale, untested, development projects, launched as a reaction to the drought. As a result, in the eyes of one observer, the people were used as guinea pigs. Of twenty-one agricultural projects of all types evaluated in 1980, only two were found to have achieved their objectives. As the experts dream up solutions to the spreading desert, the nomads are not given much say. In the 1960s and 1970s, cattle ranching was the rage. At Toukounos and Sayam in Niger, for example, huge fenced ranches were established, but herders voted with their feet. A herder's livelihood depends on being able to shift his herds to different pastures according to the weather. Staying in one place in the Sahel is not viable for a herder (unless a vastly expensive artificial irrigated environment has been created and plenty of fertilizer is available).

The fashion then shifted towards persuading herders to graze in a systematic way, improving water resources and ascribing exclusive right over lands to particular herding groups. But fixed land rights create difficulties for nomads.

Over a year several different groups traditionally exploit the same tracts of land in turn.

Now, herders in Niger's pastoral zone have been asked what kind of development help they want. In 1979, USAID in association with the government of Niger, established the Niger Range and Livestock Project. The aim was to increase livestock production by improving both human and animal health and by restoring the income of livestock owners in the pastoral zones. Nothing so unusual in that. But the project managers took the brave decision to do nothing until the nomads themselves had been asked what they needed. Two years of research by an experienced team of Nigerians and nomad experts finally produced some novel proposals.

There are no shortcuts to an aid process which seeks out the views of prospective beneficiaries first. Getting answers out of the herders was not easy. The 1973 drought had produced a harvest of academics, journalists and agency officials asking questions in the Sahel. Barely a single herder was untouched by this information-gathering machine. But few benefits resulted for the nomads, who consequently became reluctant to talk.

By reaching out to Africa's rural poor, aid agencies encounter cultural and linguistic barriers. They are often dealing with illiterate people, not used to a helping hand from the state. In our Niger example, researchers learned how nomads saw their own problems by adapting a local game played with counters and holes scooped out of the sand. Interestingly, over-grazing and desertification were not on the nomads' list. The problems were: animal and human wealth; the high price of millet in the dry season; how to build up stocks of herder-owned animals; personal credit problems which force the sale of male cattle before they have reached their top prices; and a forest service which fines herders when their goats and camels eat trees.

These are the symptoms of poverty. Tackling them may seem a roundabout way of dealing with environmental degradation, particularly when the prospective beneficiaries do not even see environmental protection as a problem. But these herders are the crucial actors. Their habits make, or stop, the desert. Their interest must be engaged in improving the habitat. Such a process starts with listening to them and proceeds through alleviating their poverty to teaching them better ways of looking after a countryside that they then feel they have a stake in. Although physical recovery from the last drought was adequate (the estimated 40 per cent fall in herd numbers has been made good) patterns of ownership have changed. Poorer nomads in the Sahel live by looking after 'entrusted cattle' – animals which belong to newly rich absentee owners, merchants, and civil servants – in return for the animals' milk alone. In parts of Mali, up to 50 per cent of the cattle are owned by such absentee non-nomads.

How can the herder's hand be strengthened? USAID decided to set up herders' associations, an idea which had been successfully used on a nearby voluntary agency experiment. Each association may be lent a small fund with which to tackle herders' problems. Pilot associations were established and the project can be considered a success. Yet even its beneficiaries have taken a hammering in the present drought. People have been forced to migrate away from the project area and unless the government shows a determination to keep the project going, it may fail.

It is clear, therefore, that aid donors can make their money produce higher returns if they will take the revolutionary step of putting credit into the hands of nomads who previously have had no access to such finance. Like any other business people, if they have no money to replace worn-out capital goods, in their case animals, their enterprise runs down. So each association is allotted a loan according to its size (usually around $6000) to be used as a revolving credit fund and also a cereal fund of about $4500, to be used to buy cereals just after harvest when they are cheapest. The whole project for five years is to cost the donor $19 million – a lot of money, but a small part of what, say, a dam would cost. The measures will cost $600 per beneficiary.

The introduction of credit, but also the possibility of money savings, should, in theory, reduce the incentive to keep as big a herd as possible because it was formerly the only sort of asset available to the nomad.

But it may be that the only satisfactory expression of wealth for this group is extra cattle ownership. Just restoring the viability of nomad life may not surmount the plain fact that there are too many people now trying to live on this land.

We have gone into this project at some length because its small-scale, beneficiary-orientated approach seems to us so much more appropriate than the large capital-intensive projects favoured in earlier development thinking. There is now a willingness amongst African governments to direct more resources to the rural sector. From countries like Malawi and Kenya, which have long emphasized their small farming sector, to those like Zimbabwe where peasant farming is growing fast, to others like Somalia where recent price liberalization has led to a 40 per cent increase in sorghum and banana production, there is a new will. This must be built on. What is required is support for this direction: a research orientation which comes up with schemes that reflect the realities of local farming, and donor assistance to help re-finance the rural sector. However, good intentions are not enough. Such an approach cuts across what has been the momentum of aid. In the next chapter we look at how aid might be adapted to this new approach.

7 The ad-hocracy

It is the anonymous 'they'. The enigmatic 'they' who are in charge. Who is 'they'? I don't know. Nobody knows. Not even 'they' themselves.

Joseph Heller, 1961

In tracing the political and economic fault line of this disaster-prone continent, the role of aid keeps reappearing. Donors and recipient governments in Africa have not set out with any single-minded plan. Rather, what is striking is how reactive and unco-ordinated policy has been. The cumulative effect of a series of ad-hoc decisions has come to be policy by default. Foreign aid is more important to the economies of Africa than it is almost anywhere else. In sub-Saharan Africa as a whole, official annual aid per person amounted to about $18 a year in 1982; in the low income semi-arid countries, aid has, since the famine in the mid-1970s, reached more than $44 a head. In this latter group of countries per capita annual income is less than $400, so by any standards aid is a major factor in economic life. Aid has steadily grown in real terms at 5 per cent a year. Aid finances 10 per cent of gross domestic investment in Africa as a whole but up to 80 per cent for the low-income semi-arid countries. In south Asia aid only amounts to $4.80 per person. Most of these states have more dynamic self-sustaining economies, able both to attract and generate capital. For them aid is only one among several sources of capital inflows. Not so in Africa.

The relative prominence of aid in Africa also comes about because at the same time that the outside world gives with one hand, it takes with the other. Commodity prices, payments for the products of the fields and mines of Africa on which national incomes are so dependent, have fallen. President Julius Nyerere of Tanzania tells of how in 1972 it took 38 tonnes of sisal to buy a 7-tonne truck; by 1982 it took 134 tonnes. The fall in the real value of copper from Zambia's mines has been 60 per cent over the last ten years. With this massive shift in the terms of trade against Africa, aid becomes an even lonelier link to the international economy. What aid has clearly not done, however, is arrest economic decline. The Sahel states are now in the grip of a new drought and famine.

There is an aid culture in many African capitals. A small African capital can have more than a hundred visiting aid missions to deal with in a year, each adding to the demands of the local embassies for reams of statistical information about the country and projects. The most capable national officials become fully tied-up dealing with the donors. There are projects where the professional man-hours devoted to monitoring and reporting on behalf of the donor exceed those devoted to implementation.

Aid has, in many cases, been misdirected. But a litany of horror stories does not amount to a conclusive case against it. Sadly, there are people who are all too ready to dismiss aid altogether on the strength of some of its failures. If the structural reasons for these failures are understood and acted upon, aid's real benefits could be unleashed more fully. Aid in Africa has been handicapped by its past. Rooted in colonial subsidies, intended to provide political leverage and distract attention from the simultaneous economic exploitation taking place, and tainted with a nine-teenth-century sense of philanthropy towards 'backward' people, modern-day aid does not have an easy parentage to live down.

Donor governments should harbour no illusions. Far from aid being charity, donor countries are getting a bargain. Western countries give 0.35 per cent of their gross national product as official aid and the eastern bloc countries give 0.18 per cent according to the Organization for Economic Co-operation and Development (OECD) estimates (which the Soviet Union challenges). But whatever the precise figure, the influence and economic opportunities that both West and East get from aid is cheap at the price.

The return is both political and economic. Alliances are made and cemented. Markets are created for the donor's manufactured goods, and indeed some international agencies spend more on goods and services from a donor country than they get in contributions. This is particularly true in the case of a country like Britain which, because of old links, can sell experts and goods to aid projects in former colonies. Both the British and French governments have preserved old connections by a judicious use of aid. The French underwrite the West African franc currency zone and continue to provide large numbers of French 'experts' and young 'co-opérants', belonging to a semi-volunteer peace corps. Frenchmen can volunteer for service abroad in exchange for doing military service at home. The British have been able to keep their presence alive in countries such as Sudan, Kenya and Zimbabwe by continuing to help with the development of sectors, such as cash crops, that they were involved in before independence.

The Americans, like other donors, have used aid as a

means of winning friends and loyalty. In 1985 the process of prizing Mozambique away from its close relationship with the Soviet Union continued with the offer of a bilateral aid programme. Extensive American aid to Somalia and Sudan, Ethiopia's two neighbours, has been part of an effort to contain Soviet influence in the Horn of Africa.

Ethiopia itself, although it has received generous emergency food aid from the United States, has not received the long-term development support it needs to rehabilitate its agricultural sector. The Americans are not prepared to go beyond short-term humanitarian help where it conflicts sharply with their political interests. Kenya, on the other hand, as a pro-western country occupying an important strategic position has received a relative abundance of aid from the United States, Britain and multilateral donors like the World Bank.

The World Bank insists on open tendering for its contracts. But many governments, despite pressure from such bodies as the OECD, tie a large portion of their aid, which has enabled Western manufacturers to gain footholds in African markets. Hence the introduction of new types of machinery such as trucks and factory equipment for which spare parts may not be easily available. The machinery may be incompatible with what is already there or be poorly suited for use in Africa. Running costs, often high, will have to be met by the African government as aid has in the past rarely covered the recurrent costs. Foreign assistance has until recently usually been limited to the initial capital costs of projects.

The Comecon countries, that is the Soviet Union and its allies, give aid with even tighter strings. Because the rouble is not an internationally convertible currency, their aid comes solely in goods and services. Tractors and technical experts are the two most visible forms. As with the

West it brings an entrée and influence far in excess of the modest outlays incurred. It appears to be deployed with a firm eye to Soviet political advantage in the region.

A great attraction of aid for all the donors is visibility. This is particularly the case in Africa where commercial flows of capital into the sub-Saharan countries are small and the general level of economic activity is low. Of the probable $5 to $6 billion net capital inflow into Africa in 1985 (about half what it was a couple of years earlier) the World Bank and the aid donors will provide the largest part. The heavy investment of the World Bank and others is vital in a continent where infrastructure is so sparse. However, projects such as highways have remained favourites, on occasions more because of their prestige than because of intrinsic merit. That African highways have a notoriously short life because of poor maintenance, has been frequently overlooked. In several West African countries, the World Bank has calculated most roads have had to be rebuilt 20–40 per cent more expensively than they should have been because of poor maintenance. As a first swipe at road-building mania the Bank itself says maintenance budgets should be increased by 25 per cent pretty much across the board. In Africa that money can only come from donors and must mean fewer new roads.

Aid does not come only in the form of money, but also in the form of experts. They have now been joined by an army of foreign relief workers involved in the famine programmes. While famine relief workers come relatively cheap, experts don't.

Cut-price younger helpers may not be better value. Africans, ranging from government officials to refugees, are often sceptical of young foreign workers. For the young foreigner it is a marvellous learning experience, an adventure of a lifetime and it is an important exercise in internationalism, but the benefits to Africa are less certain.

The experts are another matter. In return for their high fees they bring a professional competence. More and more of them have been pumped into African governments as the view takes hold in aid circles that what is missing is managerial strength. Obviously Africa could get better value out of its existing infrastructure if the latter was managed better. The continent is full of countries where the services do not run as efficiently as they should. Yet there are now more foreign experts in Africa than during the colonial period.

The inescapable conclusion of how so many good minds, both African and expatriate, could have applied themselves to such poor effect in making choices about development, is that aid must be democratized. Decisions must be opened up to those whose lives are to be affected. Development decided by collusion between technocrats and politicians in a distant city is, however careful the technical preparations, in many cases a recipe for ineffectiveness.

This lack of popular involvement in projects is mirrored by a similar reticence in the aid agencies' relations with those who back them. The aid agencies are, in many cases, not accountable to any very clear constituency. Their supporters, be they governments or individuals, have difficulty establishing how well their money is used. Often they have to rely on the agencies' own assessment of their performance. From United Nations agency to voluntary organizations these are anodyne, censored accounts which rarely hint at the catastrophes which may have occurred during a project's life. Even the internal version is designed to protect the 'face' of colleagues rather than to get at the truth. International civil servants are a privileged lot. Their careers rise or fall depending on each other's mutual esteem. They are rarely if ever exposed to the cold wind of wider public scrutiny. They are guilty for the best of motives of applying the 'we know best' approach to those who fund them as well as those they mean to help. This demeans the ability of even famine victims to help themselves and exaggerates what Western food can do to ameliorate a far deeper crisis than a crop failure. Development-hype of this sort obscures the real nature and limitations of aid.

In Africa, the myth of the white hand reaching down to help lingers. It reinforces the exclusive approach to decision making. Education of their own home publics about the importance of aid has rightly become a major activity of the agencies. In countries such as Canada, Holland, Norway and Sweden it has led to broad public support for development work. But it focuses on the disadvantages Third World economies labour under in the international system and the moral case for relieving human suffering, rather than on the operational difficulties that aid agencies and the governments in developing countries encounter. Vague theories about obligations to help and the unfairness of the world economy become a substitute for hardnosed truths about the practical difficulties of development. There is no doubting the very real public dismay as the realities of running a relief operation in Ethiopia have gradually unfolded. From October 1984 when the public alarm was sounded until January 1985 – barring a few isolated items in the media – the view prevailed that the aid agencies and the Ethiopian government could, with enough trucks and food, reach all the hungry corners of the country.

The aid agencies knew that this was a deception. But

except for those with a political commitment to the rebel movements in Eritrea and Tigre, it was not one that the agencies went out of their way to correct. This rosy version finally cracked under journalistic pressure. The image of the starving helpless Ethiopians needing nothing more than a bowl of Western food now had to be juxtaposed with that of men with guns who were not willing to put their war aside for the convenience of a famine relief operation.

Reporting real difficulties is seen by international aid agencies as an open invitation to criticism from member governments. The management of big agencies has become so politicized that staff seek to disguise the inner workings of the agency to protect its impartiality. But the price for such secrecy is ever-mounting internal levels of incompetence.

Standards of accountability vary a great deal. Most UN agencies report once a year to their governing bodies. The World Bank, however, has an executive board, whose directors, appointed by their countries, vet and approve each project. As a single World Bank programme can be bigger than the annual budget of a UN agency, obviously donors have a relatively greater interest in keeping an eye on the quality of projects.

The voluntary agencies are little better about taking those who finance them into their trust. Hence the lack of openness about the real conditions facing the relief operation in Ethiopia. Also, a fault of many aid programmes is the one-year budget. It holds up to donor publics the exciting prospect of quick change and shies away from the development reality that viable projects capable of producing durable results take years. Their effectiveness is further hampered by officials believing their best interests are served by spending that year's allocation before the year is over, whatever the real needs in the field.

Yet governmental and voluntary agencies have kept their cards close to their chest for what they would consider the best of motives; not because they want to trick the public out of its money, but because they have convinced themselves that this is the best way of securing the support that their work deserves. There is an ironic symmetry with their frequent failure to consult those they mean to help in the Third World. They leave their own supporters in the dark on the ground that confessing the difficulties would only cost them the patience and ultimately the backing of those supporters.

The agencies must break the habit of secrecy fast if aid is to become the open bridge it should be with people at both ends: giving and receiving help and drawing mutual benefit from the relationship. Aid must be opened up. Only with full disclosure to donors and full consultation with recipients is the performance of aid likely to improve.

Aid failures are often excused on the basis that to have an extra hospital building, even if it is badly utilized, is better than nothing for the recipient country. Maybe one day things will look up and the government will be able to afford to run the hospital, so goes the complacent thinking. There is always more aid money from somewhere to try again when a project fails; maybe it will work next time. Yet the large hospital in a country which does not have even functioning village-level services, the processing factory for whose products there is no market, or the dam which rapidly silts up will almost certainly involve the African government in expensive running costs before hopes are exhausted and the installation is closed. A cumulative record of failures makes fresh assistance harder and harder to get. And in the meantime, essential needs go unmet.

More important still, a lot of aid, although concessional, is not in grant form. In other words, although it is cheaper than money borrowed commercially, it still has to be repaid. Repayment periods are longer and interest rates better than those available from commercial banks. In the case of the World Bank its lending to Africa is divided between soft-loan funds from its International Development Association, which has only a nominal service charge and a grace period of ten to fifty years for repayment of the loan, and the so-called IBRD (the Bank proper) lending at advantageous rates from funds the Bank itself has raised on the money markets. Other funds come from its sister, the International Finance Corporation (IFC) which lends to the private sector, and now there is also money from the Bank's special one-off three-year $1 billion fund for sub-Saharan Africa. The EEC, the bilateral donors, the Arab funds and the African Development Bank and others, all have their own aid-mix of grant, concessional finance and export credits. In the end, Africa has to pay. At the end of 1982 its public debt was more than $48 billion.

Also hovering over the African economic scene is the International Monetary Fund (IMF). On the basis of IMF credits outstanding at the end of 1983, Africans will have to find the IMF $3.5 billion during 1985–87. No doubt further credits will be called for to help them meet these obligations, although the IMF does not reschedule its own loans, which, since the demise of the Trust Fund, are on hard terms. But these are not economies being helped through a sticky patch, which is the recognized purpose of IMF adjustment programmes. Indeed, the IMF programmes in Africa have not only proved unpopular: most have broken down since they have been inappropriate to the needs of long-term adjustment. Membership of the global economy has proved expensive for Africa. Latin American debt has caught the headlines because the sheer volume seemed to threaten the western banking structure. Sudan's debt of $9 billion may seem a trifle compared to Brazil's of about $100 billion. And because Sudan has not been a 'good risk' for quite a while, the debt it has run up has principally been with other governments, and multi-lateral agencies rather than commercial banks. Given to help, it is now a millstone severely limiting Sudan's capacity to raise fresh finance at a time when its economy has been reduced to a shambles by, amongst other things, the drought. The debt burden is eight or nine times its normal annual export earnings. The Central African Republic, Madagascar, Somalia and Zaire face almost similar levels of indebtedness.

Like a number of African countries, Sudan's debts may seem small to outsiders, but relative to their capacity to pay, they are overwhelming. Between 1973 and 1982, sub-Saharan Africa's debt increased five-fold. In the two years 1980–82, following oil price increases and a slump in world trade, Africa borrowed heavily to maintain its level of imports. It is now paying the price. Debt-service payments are expected to increase from $4.1 billion in 1981 and $9.9 billion in 1984 to $11.6 billion a year from now till 1987. This puts the few billion dollars of extra aid generated by the drought into context. The international community is taking back with one hand what it is giving with the other. When a country can no longer afford to meet the payments on its official debt, a rescheduling takes place through the mechanism of the so-called Paris club. Of the thirty-one reschedulings that had taken place by the end of 1984, twenty-three were of the debt of thirteen sub-Saharan African countries.

While debts mount, the flow of new capital into Africa is thought to have dropped sharply to about half what it was a couple of years ago. This makes it more than ever dependent on aid as the major source of funds, the financial lifeline. But, given that aid has helped pile up this mountainous debt, is it worth it?

Obviously there are those, on both left and right, who would argue not. There is a curious coincidence of view between those on the left who consider aid neo-colonialism by another name and those on the right who think it is merely a prop for corrupt élites. However, the availability of relatively low interest capital is a crucial force for development, but for it to serve this function, foreign aid must be harnessed to genuinely dynamic forces for change within the society it seeks to assist. In particular, the neglect of the rural sector needs to be reversed.

Africa's priority, even before the famine, should have been food self-sufficiency. This is clearly recognized in the Lagos Plan of Action adopted by African leaders. This is not to say that every African country should grow enough food grains to feed itself. It is improbable that countries like Botswana or Somalia could, with available levels of agricultural technology, achieve food self-sufficiency. Nevertheless both have adequate economic potential to buy grain from neighbours which can produce surpluses. What is essential is regional food self-sufficiency. Somalia has a livestock sector, which has been poorly cared for both by the government and donors, but if managed properly, it would finance food grain imports from the region.

We have examined an agricultural strategy for Africa at greater length in the last chapter. Here, our concern is with the approach and the role of aid.

Putting the rural sector first in aid plans requires a conscious effort of outreach by development agencies. Under Robert McNamara, the World Bank took important steps towards poverty-orientated rural development. It was part of a new emphasis on developing the human capital of a country as well as its conventional economic assets. But as a development bank working within political economies as it finds them and with only a small presence on the ground in most African countries, there are limits to the Bank's achievements. It is not well placed to bring about the revolution in attitudes which a restructuring of aid towards the small farmer requires. It is also much too big to have enough time for the poor and the painstaking attention to their local economy which is required if help is to be effective. As the biggest source of development finance it is vital, though, that it should follow where others lead.

The countryside must be brought back in. This requires a much more radical restructuring of aid than, say, just an extension of present rural development programmes. Too often, these are merely token efforts. In such a context, it is hadly surprising that the rural development loans themselves tend to end up benefiting the richer elements in the countryside. Chiefs and larger landowners will have an easy time securing the lion's share for themselves when the government has little heart for treating the loans as an attack on rural poverty.

The arrangements for implementing aid should shift decisively from the large programmes to smaller and more manageable projects which can be taken over locally. Modern writing about Africa shows an innate pro-government bias (in an institutional rather than a political sense). Church and mosque groups and secular agencies already provide a huge proportion of the inadequate services at village level throughout much of Africa. Government often just does not reach to the village level.

In India voluntary agencies also play a crucial role at the village level, enjoying an uneasy relationship with town-based government that has tacitly acknowledged that it is itself often less effective at delivering rural services. Although the start-up of these groups was often helped by foreign agencies, they are now Indian. A similar model should be sought for Africa. So, although there might be an initial expansion in the number of outside agency staff working at the village level, it would be temporary and should be more than off-set in cost by sending home many of the urban-based expatriate advisers.

Until now, given the scarcity of their resources, governments were flying in the face of their own political interests if they gave their major attention to the rural sector. Now with endemic crisis in the countryside, and the prospect of mounting food shortages, disaster will close in on the towns. Already, large numbers of urban poor have suffered. In cities such as Omdurman in Sudan and Nouakchott in Mauritania, there have been major influxes of dispossessed rural people. With city life threatened by the disaster in the countryside, the time is ripe for those in power to change their priorities and put the rural sector first.

As well as supporting non-governmental initiatives at the local level, they must put their own trained people back in the villages. African civil services have a congenital urban drift. Not surprisingly life is better in the cities; those serving outside too often do not get paid regularly, and they are frequently not given the resources to make an impact on the problems facing them. Their tour of duty is

114

considered exile from a desk in the national or provincial Ministry. Few, if any, governments have learned how to build a rural-based administration that effectively delivers services.

But rural communities themselves must draw their own lesson from the failure of government and international aid. They must recover an economic integrity that the market economy, however imperfectly it may operate in the countryside, has taken from them. Western Hercules planes and Soviet helicopters ferrying in supplies in Ethiopia have not changed the basic historical lesson of outside relief: it is often too little, too late.

Communities must, as they traditionally did, face up to the realities of the fragility of agriculture in Africa. There should be village-level grain reserves as a community-organized insurance against crop failure. And even if governments embrace the price rises for food crops being urged on them by the World Bank and other donors, peasants would be wise to resist selling all they have got. They need their own food insurance; they cannot count on the government. Already official statistics about food shortage have under-estimated the extent of the individual reserves farmers have kept in underground stores.

Communities should make more systematic provision against a bad harvest. Obviously, they cannot do enough to withstand several years of crop failure, but enough could be done to see them through one-year failures or until governments and the international community have gone through the slow business of mobilizing themselves to help. The crisis has shown the need for reform in the approach of governments and aid agencies. It has also shown their limits. Communities must aim for self-reliance, because in important ways they are on their own. And an aid and governmental community, which learnt the lesson of the famine, would recognize that it should stop trying to hand down development and concentrate on supporting initiatives from communities themselves. In the next chapter, we look at the turbulence which now affects rural Africa and how this complicates its relations with those who govern it.

8 Displacement and disruption

Government is a contrivance of human wisdom to provide for human wants.

Edmund Burke, 1790

Between 1957 and 1980, most of a continent which had been arbitrarily carved up between European powers in a dash for empire (sometimes commercially inspired, but often just a bewilderingly flippant imperial adventure) gained its independence. A multitude of new states emerged on the international scene. This was the last flick in the tail of formal colonialism. The manner of its going was such that it left a fragmented map of Africa where few states were viable entities. National boundaries played havoc with ethnic loyalties and created dozens of mini-states, in terms of population if not always of land area, which are not viable economically let alone politically.

The reaction of the newly independent African governments to the poor political hand they have been dealt was to decide that for better or worse the national borders they inherited should remain sacrosanct. The greatest success of the Organization of African Unity (OAU) has been its members' respect for each other's national borders. There have been countless ethnic imperatives for countries to grab at chunks of their neighbour's territory just to reunite groups split by frontiers. These have, almost all, been resisted. If they had not, the new map of Africa might have quickly unravelled. The importance of this achievement cannot be over-emphasized.

However, the price has been instability within states because ethnic minorities have had inadequate political outlet. Those groups on a state's periphery, which feel that they should have had a political entity of their own or been part of a neighbouring country's territory because of their shared links of kin, have been left out. Now some such groups are seeking change through the gun and this has become bound up with the famine. A civil war does not provide the best environment for farming!

African governments are quick to point out the imperfections of the state framework they have inherited and rightly place the blame on colonial powers. But they then choose to live rigidly by the very principle, that of the formal state structure, whose imperfections they blame on others. Whatever the political justice for this, closer attention should be paid to the humanitarian consequences.

Another consequence of the uncertain political climate is an African arms race. Africa's spending is minute compared to the more than $2 billion a day that the world as a whole spends on armaments. But as figure II shows, spending is increasing, and given the low volume of public spending (a problem common to most developing countries) it occupies a disproportionately high place in government expenditure.

It might be added that many of the major aid donors are also arms suppliers. And although to some extent these activities are coincidental, arms and aid are seen as two aspects of building strategic alliances on the continent. Responsibility for the African arms race is not Africa's alone.

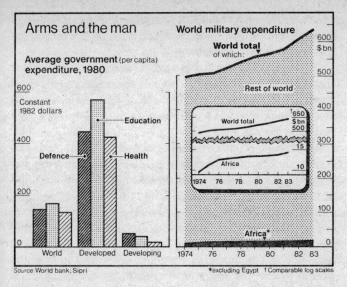

Figure II

Although development assistance is intended for non-military projects, there is the question of what is euphemistically termed 'fungibility'. This is the tendency of aid, which is provided in the form of foreign currency, to drift away from the projects for which it was intended to ones the government itself ascribes a higher priority to, but cannot find external funds for. Top of the list is often arms purchases. The donor, once funds have been handed over to a government, can only monitor the progress of the actual project, not what happens to the actual funds transferred. The fate of the cash once it has passed into the national treasury is unclear. While arms remain such a pressing priority, it is not unreasonable to assume that some portion of aid ends up financing such purchases. Even when the aid is used on the intended non-military project, it

119

may have the effect of enabling a government to free scarce resources of its own for arms which it would not otherwise have been able to afford.

So Africa, fragmented into states struggling to achieve viability, is overwhelmed partly as a consequence of this by massive migrations of people; and is shackled by governments which respond to the fragility of their authority by investing in guns.

Providing a protective shell against cross-border military actions should not allow the doctrine of national sovereignty to block the evolution of more meaningful forms of political association. Nor should it be a bar to humanitarian interventions across national borders. Men carrying grain rather than guns must be allowed across borders. Just as the Red Cross has had medical rights in war, there is now a need for a humanitarian right of access and protection where formal authority is so muddled. Where ancient ethnic rights go unprotected and unrepresented in very young nation states, humanitarian considerations should prevail over sovereign prerogatives and political considerations.

The present massive migratory movements in Africa have been triggered by crop failure, environmental deterioration, exclusion from what support the state can provide and, in some cases, active persecution. Add to this increased instability from local insurrections and the reasons for flight become pressing as well as multiple. The effects could be mitigated, as we have argued, if humanitarian intervention at source were possible before such factors come together and force large numbers of people to move.

In Sudan alone there are more than 100,000 Chadians, 700,000 Ethiopians and 250,000 Ugandans. There are also Ethiopians in Somalia, and Sudanese and Somalis in

Ethiopia. There are massive migratory movements as lands fail to hold populations in the Sahel states as well as smaller inter-state movements in Southern Africa. And above all there are massive internal movements of people within states which are not reflected in any refugee statistics. The United Nations estimates that the present crisis has created some ten million migrants.

African governments' collective attitude to the continent's refugees has gone through three phases. In the first heady days of independence, the states producing refugees were still those in the grip of white colonialism. Providing sanctuary to refugees from South Africa or Namibia united rather than divided independent Africa. In fact on the crest of this wave in 1969, Africa adopted the OAU Refugee Convention which remains a model of enlightened commitment to refugee rights.

But by the early 1980s, after the repatriation of refugees to an independent Zimbabwe, Angola, Mozambique, etc, refugees from white colonialism amounted to only about 5 per cent of Africa's caseload. Instead, the most lasting colonial legacy showed up in a second generation of refugee flows; those caused by state borders and new governments trying to impose their authority. Now without the universally acceptable scapegoat of colonialism refugees became a source of friction rather than unity. This was, and remains, particularly true in the Horn of Africa where the relations of Sudan and Somalia with Ethiopia have become bound up with the refugee flows.

By 1984, hardening attitudes, less generous asylum and even refoulements – the forced return of refugees against their will to their home countries – had become commonplace in some parts of Africa. Then the drought hit and political refugee flows became overlaid by the much larger migrations of drought victims. With this have returned more generous attitudes in the receiving countries towards the victims. A drought victim is a less contentious figure than a refugee.

But can the international community turn this to advantage, and demand, even where political and military factors are as much in the ascendant as is the case in several of the present migratory flows in Africa, that on humanitarian grounds it be allowed to intervene and bring in aid to affected populations? Where the land can support them, people can be best helped to get back on their feet and regain self-sufficiency if they are aided in the home area rather than in distant relief camps. If left to migrate to such camps they fall into total dependency on outside help.

A major force for migration is population growth. In an under-populated continent, too many people are crowded on to parched, deteriorating land. Our map V shows where population is crowded too tightly and where there is room for expansion. It is a not unreasonable guess that in time demographic pressures will cause a massive human breakout through the borders of the present state grid. The present uneven distribution cannot last.

But with their difficulty in managing the present migrations, the prospect of African governments and the international community responding effectively to much bigger flows is not promising.

Not only have new nation state frontiers disrupted traditional nomadic migration, but they now prevent much more major movements as a logical response to environmental reality. There are strong pressures for massive population relocation. The great rain forests of Zaire and the underpopulated Congo, Ivory Coast and Gabon offer space for the hard-pressed nomads and farmers perched on the ever-encroaching desert frontier of the Sahara. Gabon

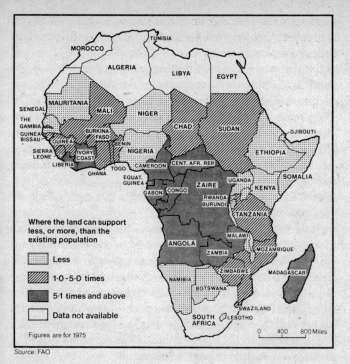

Map V

Source: FAO

has the land to support a population twenty times its present size. No doubt such population movements will export their fair share of environmental ruin with them, as tropical forests are savaged by unplanned settlement by people unused to such a terrain and not understanding the fragility of the soil base.

Almost certainly it will be people who will take the initiative to move and governments and political structures will have to follow as best they can. Government-organized migrations have a mixed record. The two most well-known current examples are in Brazil and Indonesia. Both are expensive and have a high failure rate. People drift back to where they came from.

In the past in Africa settlement schemes for drought victims, such as in Somalia, have mostly been expensive failures. The only ambitious scheme to have come out of the present drought so far is in Ethiopia. The government plans to move 1.2 million people in the next few years. Yet, however sound their reasons for doing so on environmental grounds, they do not enjoy sufficient political trust amongst many of those they are moving to make it work. Nor is it likely that they can find the funds to organize adequate facilities at the new sites.

It is more probable that population movements away from the encroaching deserts will be spontaneous and not enjoy official support. They have already started. In Sudan several million people have moved away from the arid and semi-arid areas of the west. In Mali there has been massive migration. Where the movement of those in the Sahel states will stop is still unclear. But it is probable that they will continue to seek new homes away from the threat of the desert. A sudden burst of good rain would probably no longer reverse the trend. The migrants can only go back to pick up a precarious, and in the end unsustainable life, on the encroaching desert so many times before despair sets in. There are too many people scratching a living off poor lands while elsewhere virgin lands tempt immigration. Such movements of people will be one more pressure on Africa's over-stretched governments. Unless the process is properly managed, it could cause many political and ecological problems.

9　Seeds of hope

It is better to light a candle than to curse the darkness.

Chinese proverb

The principal purpose of this report is to rescue hope from the present human tragedy. The scale of the disaster that has befallen Africa has awakened a new concern abroad to help. In Africa it has added to the urgency of the search for new directions.

The tragedy in Africa must be reversed. A new will and common purpose to do so is emerging. If these can be harnessed to practical actions for reform, the cycle of disaster that now afflicts the continent can be broken. In this final chapter we propose two areas where a series of very feasible actions can transform the prospects for rural Africa.

The victims of Africa's crisis are small farmers, both cultivators and herdsmen. At present they need external assistance to survive but they are also the key to the longer-term economic health of the continent. Unless this sector is strong, Africa's broader ambitions for development will be thwarted.

To assist them through recovery to strength, two basic institutional mechanisms are required: first, a means of securing the deployment of sufficient relief assistance early enough so as to avert, or at least contain famine; second, a way of channelling development aid directly to the small farmer who would then have a real control over its use, thereby transforming the prospects of the rural sector. But as we have argued, the growing number of the poor and the long-term decline in food production mean that Africa's vulnerability to famine is not going to be overcome overnight.

This report has not dealt with the wider international economic situation because we wished to limit ourselves to the specificity of the African situation and to plead in favour of better management of the existing African environment, social and economic as well as natural. To achieve this we make a set of proposals intended to put the rural sector first and provide appropriate assistance. As we have also pointed out, African governments have, in statements of their own, already indicated an interest in breaking with the urban bias of their present policies. The need for reform is urgent. Famine is still claiming lives. So our recommendations deliberately lie within 'the art of the possible'.

The reason for not considering in any depth the wider international economic situation is because we wished to concentrate on the African dimension of the problem. Nonetheless, several points need reiterating. Firstly, many of Africa's current problems originate in a depressed and inequitable international economy. African governments face severe limitations on their economic freedom to act. Thus, while some of the policies pursued have been ineffectual and even, in cases, counterproductive, they should not be made scapegoats for a disaster whose origins lie also in overseas economic events. A number of African governments are seeking to reform domestic policies. By contrast, no serious international economic reform is taking place.

Something, however, must be done urgently about the very high debt burden of Africa, the payments on which offset much of the new aid inflows. This ties the hands of African governments. The need for debt relief is, therefore, a priority. Because so much of it is official, as against commercial, debt it is well within the power of Western donors to reschedule the debt so as to ease the financial crisis of African governments. It is absurd that as relief aid ostentatiously flows in, it is becoming ever harder for African governments either to borrow fresh concessional finance or to pay back the mounting interest on old loans.

This general economic crisis bears on our own proposals for resolving the food production crisis. This is because it handicaps the ability of African governments to act themselves. Their urban populations have already had to bear heavy falls in living standards and governments can no longer adequately finance existing activities. So to ask them to bear the financial as well as the political burden of putting the rural poor first is unrealistic.

We cannot evade the conclusion that the richer countries of both East and West have the responsibility to help Africa with substantial concessional finance for the purpose of reconstruction and development. The ambivalent response shown to the World Bank's efforts to raise additional resources emphasizes how much more needs to be done. In the area of famine prevention and containment, much can be achieved through a redeployment of existing resources. And by ensuring that relief is available before people are forced to migrate, the relief phase will be shorter and more cost-effective. People will be back on their feet more quickly. In time our proposals for development of the rural sector will reduce the need for relief operations by making rural communities self-sufficient in food and so less vulnerable to famine.

It will become clear later in the chapter that we are proposing a fundamentally different demand-led aid for the rural sector. Rather than donors deciding on the speed and amounts in which they supply aid, the beneficiaries will, through decentralized rural credit schemes, set the level of their own demand. This will ensure that aid is only drawn on to the extent it can be successfully absorbed. And because the aid will be supplied principally as revolving credit, whereby repayments are recycled as new loans to other members of the community, a little help will go a long way. Of course, we do not underestimate the difficulties involved in rural credit schemes: high default rates; problems caused by larger landowners; shifting populations, unclear title to land, uncertain responsibility for the loan in co-operative ventures, and much more. Thus the lending conditions either have to be strict, in which case not enough will be lent or there will be repayment problems. Nevertheless, there have been encouraging successes. For example, the International Fund for Agricultural Development (IFAD) has pioneered good schemes. It has now, unfortunately, run into financial constraints because of parsimonious donors. Yet this is a model on which to build.

First, however, we turn to reform of the international community's response to disaster. The principal constraints at the moment are political and organizational. The two are interrelated. On the political side, national prerogatives are used too frequently to prevent humanitarian interventions whose purpose is to save lives. This has continued to be a serious obstacle for both bilateral and multilateral aid. The UN set-up for emergencies has often assumed the reactive character of an organization which responds only when it is formally asked to. The non-governmental character of the Red Cross movement and some individual voluntary agencies has enabled them to be more enterprising.

The first step towards enabling the UN, in particular, to establish a more pre-emptive role in disasters like famines, which can be seen building up well in advance, is for some basic principles governing such interventions to be accepted and endorsed at the regional level. The humanitarian pressure from regional powers will facilitate the UN's task in terms of access and timely aid measures in the afflicted areas. In the case of the African famine, President Julius Nyerere of Tanzania as the chairman of the Organization of African Unity has unequivocally demanded a universal right to food for all famine victims. This commitment needs, among other things, to be translated into discreet diplomatic pressure to ensure that that right is fulfilled in such areas as northern Ethiopia, Chad and Angola.

Africa is a good example of where the regional layer of internationalism has been under-used. Its growing importance is evident in the proliferation of common trading zones and other co-operative ventures between adjacent states. There are now quite successful associations of states for trade and development in western and southern Africa. Many of these smaller groupings may be able to exercise greater humanitarian pressure than the OAU itself, particularly since the anomalies of colonial boundaries mean many countries may feel close links of kinship with disaster victims in a neighbouring state.

These special interests make it important, however, to secure as clear a separation as possible of the UN's humanitarian intervention from political considerations. In its early days, a number of UN interventions did attempt to treat victims on both sides of a conflict. This was the case in post-war China, for example. It is interesting to note that the United Nations Relief and Rehabilitation Administration (UNRRA) acted in China under a resolution of its council that enabled it to distribute relief irrespective of who was controlling the territory. The relevant resolution said: '. . . that at no time shall relief and rehabilitation supplies be used as a political weapon, and no discrimination shall be made in the distribution of relief supplies because of race, creed, or political belief'. That principle is as important today as it was then.

In Africa, liberation movements have been an acceptable channel through which to pass international refugee assistance, whatever the government concerned might say. Where there is a major disaster, humanitarian considerations must override sovereign prerogatives. Bluntly the UN should be prepared to trespass on states' rights when these are in conflict with the rights of disaster victims. It is, of course, inherently difficult for an inter-governmental organization to do this. Its members should, therefore, be urged to establish a more creative humanitarian focus within the UN that ensures its considerable latent authority be deployed so that famine and other disaster victims are not left unnoticed, or uncared for, until too late. The UN, at its best, combines its moral authority with discreet diplomacy, its so-called good offices, to powerful effect. It has achieved this on occasions in its peace-keeping work and to some extent on human rights matters. It is for these reasons that the UN system needs to be supported and adapted to play a more central role on humanitarian issues. In particular, effective direction of humanitarian affairs must be vested in a body which has adequate authority and is recognizably non-political.

On disasters in general, the Office of the UN Disaster Relief Co-ordinator (UNDRO) was expected to take the lead within the UN system. It has not been able to do so, partly because it lacked both authority and finance. Disaster prevention, which is a part of its mandate, calls for innovative pre-disaster planning and intervention. The fact that the UN Secretary General has had to form an office for emergency operations in Africa, as indeed he has done in virtually all other major emergencies, is a clear indication of present shortcomings.

The powerful UN agencies, with sectoral responsibilities of their own from refugees to food and health care, have never really acknowledged its co-ordination. UNDRO is a small under-financed office in Geneva. Effective direction of humanitarian affairs must be lodged in an office with adequate authority and a clearly recognized non-political character.

Information gathering must not remain solely a post-disaster activity but should include early warning. A network of voluntary agencies and others to monitor famine indicators, such as food and livestock prices, in vulnerable areas in the developing world would be an important component of this. The UN Secretary General has begun to improve the monitoring of potential conflict areas on the basis of published information. For humanitarian emergencies, a more extensive grass-roots exercise in information gathering is needed.

The purpose of any organizational change would not be the creation of another international bureaucracy but the more effective use of existing resources. Not all aid operations take place in a difficult political context where help cannot get through to all victims. In many cases the famine victims go unfed because the relief operation is simply not well-enough run. Because of widespread disillusion with the performance of the multilateral system an increasing amount of relief aid during the African famine is being delivered by the bilateral donors and the voluntary agencies themselves. However, as we have argued the United Nations has an 'entrée' where others might be refused access even when there are no political complications.

One way of strengthening the UN's capacity would be to establish its own logistics agency to move relief goods to where they are needed. A number of countries which have built up their own disaster corps, such as Sweden and Switzerland, may be invited to wear a UN hat and operate more or less as do the UN peace-keeping forces.

Multilateral and bilateral aid systems should be complementary, not competitive. Problems of duplication should be addressed through a control mechanism as suggested above. Greater efforts should also be made to engage the socialist countries more fully in what should be a concerted effort in a purely humanitarian context.

A more effective role should be accorded to voluntary agencies. Many combine a cost-effective operational capacity with the support of a public constituency in the donor countries. Both are vital. The voluntary agencies do not alone, however, offer an aid panacea. Their strength is their smallness and diversity, which would be lost if they had to carry the whole burden of aid delivery alone. They must remain the innovative partners and vanguard within the aid community as a whole, trend-setters and catalysts. Making them as big as the UN would destroy their main asset.

Better relief, however, only limits the consequences of Africa's vulnerability. The major thrust must be a longer-term re-establishing of a rural economy where the risk of famine is sharply reduced. As we have argued, this requires restoring traditional agriculture, encouraging improvements that fit within environmental limits. Modern agricultural methods have in many cases speeded up the pace of environmental deterioration.

The agricultural trends in recent decades have not only created environmental damage in their own right but played a part in impoverishing the small scale farming sector. Together with increased population pressure and other economic changes, including the lasting impact of famine, the small-scale farming sector is now under-funded, even by its own modest standards. And in the Sahel states, western Sudan and northern Ethiopia particularly, a living is being scratched off land which can no longer carry the existing population. People in many areas have to walk too far for water or firewood for the family farming unit to be productive.

Turning this situation around will require a package of environmental and agricultural measures that we have discussed in earlier chapters. Here we limit ourselves to a mechanism for achieving this. There is a lot of well-intentioned exhortation to put the peasant first in development policy in Africa; but the biases of aid experts in favour of articulate townspeople and the urban political imperatives of governments make it unlikely that a strategic shift can take place easily.

One of the institutional arrangements which we believe could put power back into the hands of small farmers is the provision of decentralized low-cost risk capital. The small farmer is under-financed both in general but also seasonally. Not only are basic inputs such as seeds often unaffordable (or unavailable) but the consequence of rural poverty and indebtedness is that without credit the farmer has to sell his crop as soon as it is harvested when prices are at their lowest. The livestock herdsman is in a similar position.

The remarkable performance of Chinese peasants in

recent years, who have been increasing wheat production at 12 per cent a year, is an example of what an economically liberated peasantry can achieve. In the African context, the performance of countries such as Ivory Coast, Kenya, Malawi, Rwanda and Zimbabwe are all encouraging examples. But unlike many, we doubt that raising food prices will be incentive enough for increased food production.

Reportedly, as much as 75 per cent of the basic grains grown by small farmers in Africa never leave the village. This is largely because the market system is so underdeveloped. Major improvements in rural transport and the phasing out of urban dependence on foreign food imports, which are often easier and cheaper to get, are crucial. The decision of a number of African governments to diminish the role of state marketing boards in setting prices is important. These boards are now criticized for holding food prices artificially low. However, they were set up because one or two merchants could in the past dominate the market to the benefit of neither the food producers nor the consumers. Yet the boards have generally not lived up to their purpose. Inefficient management, coupled on occasion with corruption, have brought them low. Whatever marketing arrangements are adopted, the small farmer's access to market on fair terms must be protected.

It is not consumers who have been starving during the present famine, it is producer-consumers, the peasant farmers themselves who, whether or not they thought the price was right to grow a surplus for market, would certainly have tried to grow what they could for their own needs. So while growing a surplus for market will be an important consequence of making credit available to rural producers, the first consequence is likely to be that their own food security will improve. They will keep more to eat themselves.

However, a credit scheme will draw peasant farmers further into a money economy. They will have to pay back what they have borrowed. In some cases if there are not realistic opportunities to sell their produce to make such payments, the scheme might take payment in kind, in grains or livestock, because obviously the purpose is not to increase the burden of rural debt. But in most instances low-interest repayments into a revolving fund to help other members of the community will be possible.

Peasant farming, when properly financed and with adequate access to markets, is one of the best banking risks around. Where appropriate this link-up with local capital might be facilitated if donors are willing to provide collateral for African banks to run such schemes.

Credit must be promoted because the one common aspect of the crisis in the African countryside is the impoverishment of the small farmer. But equally credit is the answer because, impoverishment apart, no two agricultural communities are the same. No top-down agricultural theories will work. Development aid has to have built into it an adaptability to the community with which it interacts. Credit will give the community the dominant say over how financial resources are used.

But at least in the early stages the majority of such schemes should be run at the local level by voluntary agencies and others familiar with particular communities. There has been considerable experimentation with such funds in Africa and elsewhere. IFAD, which specializes in rural credit schemes, now has a special programme for Africa. However, what is crucial for the success of rural credit is that a scheme is structured with the particular needs, opportunities and character of a community in mind. Obviously, a poorly executed scheme could enrich the leaders of a community and pass others by. After all, credit favours the risk-takers: often only the rich can afford risks. Or if land rights are required as security for a loan, women who head most farming households in Africa may be excluded because traditionally these rights have rested with the men. Successful schemes will almost certainly have some co-operative element to them, not just because of the revolving fund but because there are common needs such as warehousing.

A plausible channel for credit is an indigenous local group, which understands the local power structures and the needs, and which co-operatively borrows the money and manages the loans to individuals. An international aid agency can identify such groups, guarantee collateral to a local bank to allow them to make such loans, and then provide the group with whatever expertise, research or other help it requires.

So, it becomes crucial to encourage the growth of local voluntary groups committed to the rural sector. These will provide an indigenous channel for aid and may as they gather strength become a legitimate voice for rural interests, listened to and tolerated by governments in a way political organizations at the grass roots could not be.

Credit must be wedded through these community-based agencies to the continued provision of more traditional forms of assistance which build up the human capital of the community with the provision of schools and clinics and so on. Agricultural extension services must be improved so that farmers have useful relevant advice at their disposal. The main attraction of credit is that used intelligently it gives the borrower a power over its use which as a beneficiary of free aid, he, or she, never has. The farmer can choose what advice to take and what to ignore. Getting aid is no longer tied to doing what the 'experts' tell you. This, in turn, gives Africa a chance to recoup traditional farming wisdom and allow a more balanced marriage with new productivity-raising methods.

Obviously such schemes have to be ultra-sensitive to local realities if they are not to be exploited by the richer farmers. So rather than offering a single institutional blueprint, we propose that those with aid programmes in Africa take a conscious decision to allocate a fixed proportion of their funds to rural credit schemes. By definition the cumulative impact of these funds, recycled between borrowers whose economic prospects could be so much better than those in the urban sector, is likely to exceed that of other parts of a donor's aid programme.

Famine begins as a local crisis. It develops when acute food shortage remains unattended to and is only acknowledged outside the community when it achieves a wider dimension involving death and disruption. What is astonishing is that the slow-burning fuse of food crisis, with its series of community-level crises from soaring prices in the local market to forced migration of the destitute, should remain virtually invisible at the national and international level until widespread starvation breaks out.

The fact that counter-measures are not taken sooner goes to the heart of what is wrong with the development process. The urban orientation of government, and the virtual exclusion of the rural sector from resources and power, has led to the impoverishment and vulnerability that brings about famine.

Restoring local self-reliance requires a restructuring of government policies and international aid so that they serve the interests of the rural majority in Africa more effectively. In particular the rural poor, the current famine victims, must be economically enfranchised. Aid should be channelled to this group, principally in the form of low-cost credit. Such an approach, based on self-help, will provide incentive, restore human dignity and eliminate overtones of charity.

Taken together with improved price incentives for food production, there is then a real prospect of rebuilding small scale agriculture. Furthermore, such an agriculture understands the limits of its environment. When we raise the question of whether famine is man-made, we are not denying the role of climate in Africa. We are only emphasizing that in the past, people knew how to farm within Africa's severe ecological limits and to take the precaution of ensuring that there was enough food stocked in the village for the years of bad harvests. It is this sort of wisdom which must not be lost.

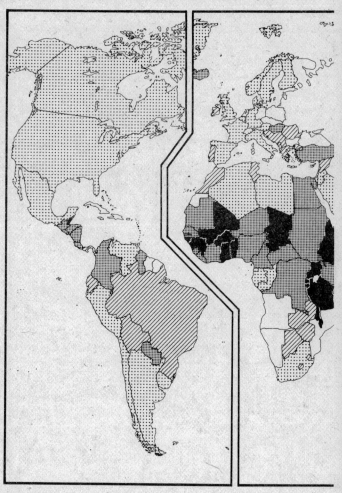

Map VI

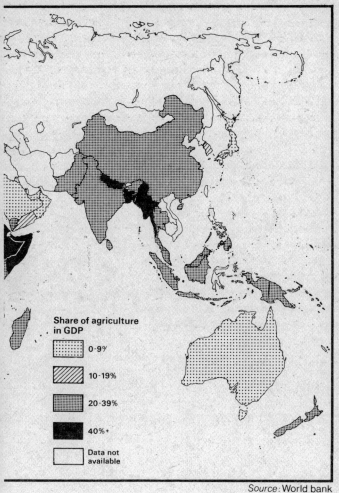

Share of agriculture in GDP

0-9%

10-19%

20-39%

40%+

Data not available

Source: World bank

Appendix 1:
Communiqué: situation in Africa

Adopted by consensus at the ICIHI Plenary Meeting
Tunisia, May 1984

At the meeting in Tunisia of the Independent Commission on International Humanitarian Issues – its first plenary session in Africa – Prime Minister Mzali, a member of the Commission, said in his opening statement that the African continent, the cradle of the first human beings on earth, has now fallen prey to a series of disastrous calamities. There was a serious risk that the much-desired development would be overtaken by ruination.

Profound concern was expressed at the meeting for the humanitarian consequences of the grave crisis unfolding on the African continent. The magnitude of the crisis demands the most urgent response from the international community to buttress the efforts of all African governments in seeking solutions to the crisis and in combating its dire consequences.

The extent of the problem is such that hardly a country on the continent has been left untouched by the cycle of poverty, hunger, disease and degradation of the environment. It is estimated that in 1984 five million infants alone will die in Africa.

The humanitarian crisis in Africa does not stem from a single cause, nor are its solutions to be found in a simple formula. Its roots lie in a complex interaction between external and internal forces. The international economic environment has severely, and in some cases decisively, compounded Africa's poverty and neutralized much of the development efforts made by African governments and peoples over the last three decades. High energy prices, high interest rates, declining terms of trade, growing protectionism and debilitating debt burdens have diminished the resilience of African economies. Exacerbating Africa's present precarious situation is the immediate threat to the IDA's funds and other relevant programmes of the World Bank on which Africa's poorest countries rely – a threat resulting directly from the policies adopted by some of the richest countries. The predicament faced by the IDA is a major and unwarranted blow to Africa at a time of its greatest need. Similarly, IMF policies have been insensitive to Africa's current financial problems, most of which stem from factors far beyond the control of African governments.

Ultimately, only Africans can devise solutions for the problems of Africa. Dissension within and among African states has generated massive humanitarian problems directly, and indirectly through its negative impact of development efforts. Response to, or preparation for, armed conflicts has led to a disproportionate investment of scarce resources in armaments. The best interests of African peoples also demand a forthright approach to internal problems of economic mismanagement and corruption. An improvement in the current situation depends on a determined strategy, pioneered by Africans for Africans and supported by the international community, to combat poverty.

Our sense of common humanity demands the recognition that the daunting problems faced by Africa are not Africa's alone – whether in their making, their implications, or in the solutions that must be found to them. They are problems which Africa shares with the world. Global co-operation in meeting them is not peripheral but central to the survival of millions of human beings, and is also a test of international commitment to humanitarian values.

The Commission is acutely conscious of the colossal problems being faced by many countries due to the massive movements of populations, refugees and displaced persons as well as the problems of armed conflicts in many areas. However, at this stage of its work, the Commission has concentrated primarily on basic needs and the effects of drought and desertification on African life. Our conclusions are at once grave and serious.

We have noted that continuous and widespread drought, exacerbated by the mismanagement of the range ecology, have ensured that virtually the whole of Africa is engaged in a struggle for survival. Rainfall in parts of Western Africa is at its lowest point for half a century. Drought is now a permanent feature in some countries as they enter their tenth year without rain.

Acute food shortages are endemic in half the countries of Africa. Over 150 million people face mass starvation and an accelerating decline in their standard of living. Food production per person has fallen on average by 11 per cent since 1970. As economies continue to deteriorate, hunger and malnutrition become endemic.

Extensive bush fires have accompanied the drought in many areas. These destroy not only people's homes and villages, but irreplaceable plants, trees and animals – that is, the inherited genetic stock of a region – adding a serious ecological twist to the disaster. The loss of African top soil is more serious than anywhere else in the world, and in West Africa has led already to a reduction in corn yields of 52 per cent, and in legumes of 38 per cent.

Moreover, in some areas savage flooding, following drought, has devastated remaining crops and destroyed the local infrastructure. Thousands of families have been uprooted as a consequence.

The vicious, downward spiral thus unleashed is accelerating. Shortly it could be out of control. The strain created accelerates the collapse of traditional societies.

Food and water remain key components for all African communities. But for many farmers, seeds for the 1984 harvest have already been eaten, as the only means to immediate survival. Where seeds are available, they are often beyond the purchasing power of the farmer; available funds for fertilizers, well-digging, agricultural production and animal husbandry are no longer adequate; people are migrating from drought-stricken areas to overcrowded camps, villages or towns in adjacent areas, regardless of national boundaries, or the inability of the area to cope with the massive influx of new populations. The status and future of these people remain unclear.

The hardship being endured is at high human cost. It has been estimated that five million infants alone will die in Africa in 1984. Physically and mentally, millions of African children will be adversely affected, for life, as a result of their experience over the last five years. For those who have survived, genetic changes resulting from malnutrition in pre- and immediate post-natal babies, may be passed on, through the female child, to the unborn of the future.

At most, only a quarter of the people of Africa have access to safe drinking water, so that water-borne diseases continue to afflict the majority. Even fewer people have access to preventative health-care programmes, resulting in malnutrition, high infant mortality and low life expectancy.

As if these afflictions were not enough to debilitate the most resilient of societies, stagnant economies and high population growth, including the highest fertility rate in the world, ensure that per-capita income is less now than it was ten years ago, in many of Africa's poorer countries.

In parts of Africa only half the urban labour force is employed and in the last five years trade has declined by some 50 per cent. The inevitable loss of foreign earnings, is equivalent to the total aid received by the continent – the one making a mockery of the other. The fall in commodity prices is little short of calamitous whilst the cost of servicing debt, last year, south of the Sahara, is estimated to have increased by 60 per cent. Elsewhere, increases in excess of 25 per cent are not unusual. 1984 will see a further deterioration of present trends.

Meanwhile, armed conflicts and violence, in certain parts of Africa, add unnecessary bloodshed and turmoil to a tragic situation. Indeed the spread of militarism throughout the continent, and disproportionate spending by many African governments on armaments and sophisticated defence systems, constantly drain scarce resources from human development. Priority is given to weapons of destruction, when people need hoes and seeds to grow food, clean water to drink and simple, low-cost preventive health programmes. Militarism is perpetuated and costly armies maintained, when the priority should be economic and political stability based on a harmonious, self-reliant population.

All of this represents an immense humanitarian challenge of global proportions. People are forced into sub-human conditions to secure minimum survival levels. Frequently they fail and die. Can the rest of the world simply stand by, watching on its television screens, an entire continent collapse, economically and ecologically, and within a social environment which embraces such widespread human suffering?

We call on the world community to co-operate with the people of Africa and their governments to undertake the following measures which we offer as some of the paths towards development:

Short-term

a *Carefully controlled and managed food aid, where applicable, with a predetermined and finite life span,* should be sent to the most stricken areas immediately. Such relief programmes should be designed to encourage development and not dampen local food production. The cost of transporting food aid is beyond the capacity of many African governments, especially the land-locked Least Developed Countries. It is essential, therefore, that donor agencies bear these costs themselves, together with the costs of setting up strategically placed *local food storage depots*. These will need, in turn, to be supported by *depots for spare parts*, and fuel for trucks, trains and other means of mechanical transport. There is evidence that the suffering of the people, and the steady rise in death from starvation, is aggravated by the closure, or erratic use of key roads, railways or port facilities. Our common humanity demands that all such facilities should be opened to ease the flow of aid and trade.

b The provision of *improved pricing structures and additional credit facilities* to small scale-farmers to enable them to buy good-quality seeds, tools and fertilizers, and to improve the management of local water and irrigation schemes.

c *The debts* owed by most African countries, though small in absolute terms, impose on them burdens as onerous in terms of their own economies, as those of the major debtor countries. This problem demands the most urgent consideration by the international financial community.

d Oil-producing countries should take the initiative in negotiating a minimum five-year agreement to supply *oil at special prices* advantageous to the twenty-four worst hit countries of Africa.

Long-term

a In co-operation with the research institutions of the Consultative Group on International Agriculture Research, a *comprehensive African cereal, vegetable and fruit gene bank* should be established on the continent as a major facility so that the rich genetic diversity in Africa, including wild species, can be stored, classified and regenerated true to type, for use primarily by African plant breeders, but linked to world conservation strategies through the international data bank system of FAO and the global policies of the International Board of Plant Genetic Resources.

b *Anti-desertification* plans, based on small-scale, community-orientated, social-development schemes, should be implemented on a regional basis. Africans have successfully implemented many agroforestry tree and crop programmes, as well as effective micro-catchment water projects, particularly in the Upper Volta, Niger, Algeria, Morocco and Senegal. These should be studied and replicated systematically, as feasible, across the continent.

c In respect of the critical loss of top soil, African governments should commission regionally based research to:

i Quantify and evaluate *loss of top soil* and the cost effect of this on food production, and the silting up of rivers, deltas and harbours.

ii Study and introduce where applicable techniques of

minimum tillage, together with contour farming, agroforestry and other well established anti-desertification techniques.

iii In co-operation with the International Council for Research in Agroforestry, establish regional centres for *applied research into agroforestry* and tree cropping applicable to given geographical territories.

Whilst many Africans in the past had learned to live in harmony with their natural habitat, no effective measures have been taken by governments to make their people aware of the long-term cost to a nation's economy of the loss of top soil, or the direct link between reduced productivity and soil erosion. What is at stake here is not merely the degradation of the soil – but the degradation of life itself.

d *Tree planting* should be a national priority in every African country. School children, university undergraduates and similar groups including the army could co-operate in maintaining the momentum. Support from the specialized agencies of the UN, the World Bank and NGOs, is essential if funding and specialized techniques are to be used to optimum advantage. Extension services at village level should feature prominently in regional strategies, with ownership of the trees clearly falling to village people.

e *Preventive health-care* schemes also should be a priority for all countries. The links between nutrition, sanitation, hygiene, clean water and health, should be taught to people at village level. UN and NGO donor agencies have a major supporting role to play in encouraging this development.

f More attention and support to *production, storage and marketing* of food for local consumption; long-term pricing policies, designed to encourage production, should be studied and implemented. Increased resources should be dedicated to agricultural research and to the provision of the necessary infrastructure to support increased food production. Emphasis on monoculture, production for export markets and energy-intensive cultivation must be carefully considered in the light of local consumption patterns and needs.

g Finally, but most importantly, *people must be party to resolving their own problems* and help in the process of designing the schemes which will lead to their resolution. Self-reliance cannot be imposed from the top, but leadership can ensure that the innate skills, knowledge and resilience of the people are harnessed to combat the causes of poverty. This will not become a dynamic process across the face of Africa unless literacy levels are raised dramatically. *Mass literacy campaigns* at village level, which aim to motivate rural communities to understand their key role in maintaining a balanced range ecology, and drawing on traditional African methods, are essential.

Communiqué: situation in Africa

Adopted by consensus at the ICIHI Plenary Meeting
The Hague, Netherlands, December 1984

The Independent Commission on International Humanitarian Issues, in concluding its plenary meeting at the Hague, described the current famine in Africa as one of the greatest humanitarian tragedies in history. It warned that disasters of similar or even greater magnitude will certainly occur, in Africa and elsewhere, unless the short-term relief efforts of today are translated into long-term development programmes that address the underlying causes of the crises.

The Independent Commission, composed of twenty-six members from as many countries, found some encouragement in the outpouring of money and goods from many countries for the relief effort in Africa. But a genuine humanitarian response requires more than simply tiding the affected people over until the next harvest.

The Commissioners emphasized that the drought and famine that threaten more than thirty countries and as many as thirty-five million people in Africa are not simply caprices of nature. Long-term processes of deforestation and desertification have been set in motion by economic policies that at best neglected and at worst disrupted the productivity of traditional farming systems. Less than 25 per cent of the external aid that went to the eight Sahel countries between 1975 and 1980 was spent on agriculture, which left the entire region vulnerable to a repetition and continuation of drought-related crisis.

Governments and their agencies have not yet succeeded in channelling adequate assistance to the rural poor, whose direct participation in development efforts is an essential ingredient for progress. There is a growing realization that large-scale, capital-intensive aid projects have not resolved the basic problems of Africa. Small-scale people-orientated programmes, focused on the village unit and building upon local resources, are more likely to help that continent out of its current crisis.

Designing and implementing a people-orientated development strategy is no easy task. It requires a change of direction, a commitment of financial resources and a great deal of perseverance.

In the course of 1985, millions of African children are likely to die of hunger-related causes. The immediate urgency of saving these children and their families tends to obscure the fact that the survivors of this crisis will inherit a massively degraded environment, barely capable of supporting them without extensive rehabilitation.

The present drought, and the encroachment of the desert on to previously arable lands, is not simply the handiwork of nature. It is equally a consequence of human activity. The felling of trees in the relentless quest for firewood, the overgrazing by livestock of delicate grassy plains, the pressures of burgeoning populations, the continuance of destructive agricultural practices – all these have contributed to desertification. All have altered substantially the normal patterns of rainfall. As a result, much of Africa now faces an uncertain and hazardous future.

To reverse these deteriorating ecological conditions will demand the efforts of governments within Africa and outside of it for a half-century or more. In this task, African governments must design and pursue agricultural and population policies which reflect the needs, cultures and environmental conditions in Africa. Governments of affluent nations must allocate the resources needed to help reform agricultural practices, restore wooded areas, and to provide the infrastructure essential for food storage and distribution.

Hand in hand with such steps, techniques must be set in place which will permit early anticipation of food shortages, in order that preventive measures can be implemented and assistance organized and co-ordinated in a timely fashion. All of these measures demand sustained support and financial commitment. This commitment, however, must be measured against our painful awareness of the desperate plight of our fellow humans.

Six months ago the ICIHI advised on the impending crisis in Africa. It has undertaken a number of studies to understand better the causes of these events and the possibilities of reversing them. It is also supporting a research project that will develop and test an early warning system for famine prediction, based on local food prices and other social indicators.

It now calls on all people, governments and institutions, to respond generously to the immediate needs of Africa and to understand and support with patience the long-term developmental exercise to permit Africans to regain food self-sufficiency.

Appendix 2:
Information note on the Independent Commission on International Humanitarian Issues

The establishment of an Independent Commission on International Humanitarian Issues is the response of a group of eminent persons from all parts of the world to the deeply felt need to enhance public awareness of important humanitarian issues and to promote an international climate favouring progress in the humanitarian field.

The work of the Commission is intended to be a part of the continuing search of the world community for a more adequate international framework to uphold human dignity and rise to the challenge of colossal humanitarian problems arising with increasing frequency in all continents.

In 1981, the UN General Assembly adopted by consensus a resolution relating to a 'new international humanitarian order' in which it recognized: 'the importance of further improving a comprehensive international framework which takes fully into account existing instruments relating to humanitarian questions as well as the need for addressing those aspects which are not yet adequately covered'. In doing so, the Assembly bore in mind that 'institutional arrangements and actions of governmental and non-governmental bodies might need to be further strengthened to respond effectively in situations requiring humanitarian action'.

The following year, the General Assembly adopted by consensus a further resolution relating to the International Humanitarian Order noting 'the proposal for establishment, outside the United Nations framework, of an "Independent Commission on International Humanitarian Issues" composed of leading personalities in the humanitarian field or having wide experience of government or world affairs'.

The Independent Commission on International Humanitarian Issues was inaugurated in July 1983 and held its first plenary meeting in New York in November 1983. A few days later, the UN General Assembly adopted another resolution in which it noted the establishment of the Commission and requested the Secretary General to remain in contact with governments as well as with the Independent Commission in order to provide a comprehensive report on the humanitarian order to the Assembly in 1985. The Commission expects to hold its last plenary meeting by November 1986.

Composition of the Commission

The Commission is an independent body whose members participate in their personal capacity and not as representatives of governments or international bodies to which they may belong. Its work is not intended to interfere with governmental negotiations or inter-state relations nor to duplicate work being done by existing governmental or non-governmental international bodies.

In its deliberations, the Commission seeks to benefit from the advice of governments, existing international governmental and non-governmental bodies and leading experts. Its composition, which is intended to remain limited, is based on equitable geographical distribution. At present, the Commission has twenty-six members. Details are provided below. Its life span is three years and its final report will be issued in 1986.

Programme of work

During its limited life span of three years, 1983–86, the Commission will deal with a wide range of subjects relating to humanitarian issues of relevance to contemporary society. Its conclusions and recommendations will be based largely on in-depth studies of selected subjects carried out with the help of recognized experts and national or international bodies, chosen from all parts of the world for their specialized knowledge or experience. In addition to direct input by experts in the form of policy-orientated research papers, the Commission also sponsors panel discussions or brainstorming sessions. Similarly, close contact is maintained with agencies dealing with subjects of interest to the Commission, in order to avoid duplication of effort and strengthen the Commission's role of complementarity to the ongoing efforts and its catalytic role for innovative purposes. Heads of these agencies, or their representatives, are invited to testify at the Commission's plenary sessions.

The in-depth studies and expert advice received by the Commission will also help in the preparation of sectoral statements, to be made public occasionally in order to encourage follow-up action which may be initiated within the lifespan of the Commission. These sectoral reports will be addressed, in the first place, to policy-makers within governments, regional bodies as well as inter-governmental and private voluntary agencies. The overall effort of the Commission will thus be a pyramid-like process culminating in the final report at the end of 1986.

The main areas selected by the Independent Commission for study are:

i Humanitarian norms in the context of armed conflicts.

ii Natural and man-made disasters.

iii Vulnerable groups requiring special care and protection such as refugees and displaced persons, stateless persons, children and youth, indigenous populations, etc.

Members of the Commission

Sadruddin AGA KHAN (Iran) – Special Consultant to the Secretary General of the United Nations since 1978. Former UN High Commissioner for Refugees (1965–77).

Susanna AGNELLI (Italy) – Under-Secretary of State for Foreign Affairs since 1982. Member of Italian Parliament since 1976 and of the European Parliament from 1979–81.

Talal Bin Abdul Aziz AL SAUD (Saudi Arabia) – President of the Arab Gulf Programme for the United Nations Development Organizations (AGFUND). Former Minister of Communications and of Finance and National Economy.

Paulo Evaristo ARNS (Brazil) – Cardinal Archbishop of Sao Paulo. Chancellor of the Pontifical Catholic University in the State of Sao Paulo.

Mohammed BEDJAOUI (Algeria) – Judge at the International Court of Justice in The Hague since 1982. Former Minister of Justice. Algeria's Ambassador to France, UNESCO and the United Nations in New York.

Henrik BEER (Sweden) – Former Secretary General of the League of Red Cross Societies (1960–82). Former Secretary General of the Swedish Red Cross.

Luis ECHEVERRIA ALVAREZ (Mexico) – Former President of Mexico (1970–75). Mexican Ambassador to

Australia and New Zealand. Delegate of Mexico to UNESCO.

Pierre GRABER (Switzerland) – Former President of the Confederation and former Foreign Minister and President of the Diplomatic Conference on Humanitarian Law.

Ivan HEAD (Canada) – President of the International Development Research Centre, Canada. Served as Special Assistant to the Prime Minister (1968–78).

M. HIDAYATULLAH (India) – Former Vice-President of India, former Chief Justice of the Supreme Court.

Aziza SOUKRY HUSSEIN (Egypt) – President of the International Planned Parenthood Federation.

Manfred LACHS (Poland) – Judge of the International Court of Justice, The Hague. Served as its President (1973–76). Professor of political science.

Robert S. McNAMARA (United States) – Former Defense Secretary (1961–68). Former President of the World Bank (1968–80).

Lazar MOJSOV (Yugoslavia) – Member of the Presidency of the Socialist Federal Republic of Yugoslavia, former Federal Secretary for Foreign Affairs, President of the UN General Assembly (32nd session).

Mohamed MZALI (Tunisia) – Prime Minister. Formerly Minister of National Defence, Education, Youth and Sports and Health.

Sadako OGATA (Japan) – Diplomat, Professor, Institute of International Relations for Advanced Studies on Peace and Development in Asia.

David OWEN (United Kingdom) – Member of Parliament since 1966, leader of the Social Democratic Party. Former Foreign Secretary, former Minister of State for Health and Social Security.

Willibald PAHR (Austria) – Ambassador, former Foreign Minister (until 1983).

Shridath SURENDRANATH RAMPHAL (Guyana) – Secretary General of the Commonwealth. Former Attorney-General, Foreign and Justice Minister.

Salim AHMED SALIM (Tanzania) – Prime Minister. Former Foreign Minister; President of the United Nations General Assembly (34th session).

Leopold SEDAR SENGHOR (Senegal) – Former President of the Republic. Member of the French Academy. Poet and philosopher.

SOEDJATMOKO (Indonesia) – Rector of the United Nations University, Tokyo. Former Ambassador.

Hassan BIN TALAL (Jordan) – Crown Prince of the Hashemite Kingdom of Jordan. Founder of the Royal Scientific Society of Jordan and the Arab Thought Forum.

Simone VEIL (France) – Member and former President of the European Parliament. Former Minister of Health and Family Affairs.

Gough WHITLAM (Australia) – Ambassador to UNESCO. Former Prime Minister and Minister for Foreign Affairs.